CREATING THE CONDITIONS FOR SCHOOL IMPROVEMENT

A HANDBOOK OF STAFF DEVELOPMENT ACTIVITIES

Second Edition

MEL AINSCOW
JOHN BERESFORD
ALMA HARRIS
DAVID HOPKINS
GEOFF SOUTHWORTH
MEL WEST

David Fulton Publishers
London

David Fulton Publishers Ltd
The Chiswick Centre, 414 Chiswick High Road, London W4 5TF
www.fultonpublishers.co.uk

First published in Great Britain in 1994 by David Fulton Publishers

Note: The rights of Mel Ainscow, John Beresford, Alma Harris, David Hopkins,
Geoff Southworth and Mel West to be identified as the authors of this work
have been asserted by them in accordance with the Copyright, Designs and
Patents Act 1988.

David Fulton Publishers is a division of Granada Learning Limited, part of
Granada plc.

Copyright © David Fulton Publishers 2000

British Library Cataloguing in Publication Data
A catalogue record for this book is available from the British Library.

ISBN 1-85346-648-4

Typeset by FiSH Books, London
Printed and bound in Great Britain

Contents

Acknowledgements

Our journey of school improvement is in its 10th year, and we have enjoyed well over 100 schools as fellow travellers. The IQEA (Improving The Quality of Education for All) Project has spread from its origins in East Anglia and north London to involve schools in the East Midlands, Humberside and South Wales. IQEA hybrids have been developed in Bedfordshire, and overseas in South Africa, Puerto Rica and Scandinavia. A further project is planned in Hong Kong. Not only do we continue to learn from the teachers in our project schools, we increasingly use them to disseminate good practice across our extensive network.

Since the first edition of this book, we have all departed from what is now the Cambridge School of Education. The IQEA name lives on at Nottingham University, where new colleagues have been recruited. While they have embraced much of the IQEA philosophy and approach to school improvement, their fresh insights have enriched our work. We thank Alma Harris, Mark Hadfield, David Jackson, Colette Singleton and John Beresford for their contributions to the ongoing debate within our ranks. We also thank Hilary Stokes for organising often disparate strands into a near cohesive whole, and for helping to keep IQEA on track and on task. We feel we should give a special mention to Ruth Watts and her colleagues at Swanwick Hall, not only for their enthusiastic support of IQEA but also their unflagging energy in taking their expertise, on behalf of IQEA, to teachers in far-flung parts of England and Wales.

In preparing this school improvement handbook, we have inevitably drawn on other of our published work which we acknowledge here. In particular more detailed descriptions of the IQEA process and the school-based examples outlined in Chapters 2 and 9 are found in *School Improvement in an Era of Change* (Hopkins *et al.*, 1994). The activity on commitment and control over change in Chapter 5 and the Conditions of School Rating Scale in the Appendix are both adapted from *Mapping Change in Schools: The Cambridge Manual of Research Techniques* (Ainscow *et al.*, 1994). Similarly, the treatment of development planning in Chapters 4 and 9 is based on ideas more fully explored in *The Empowered School* (Hargreaves and Hopkins, 1991) and the DES (1989) document *Planning for School Development*.

Finally, we thank David Fulton and John Owens of David Fulton Publishers for their continued belief in our work, and their ongoing tolerance of our predilection for missing deadlines. It is their idea to reproduce this book in its present format. We hope you share their belief, and those of the writers, that the book is as relevant today as it was in 1994.

Mel Ainscow and Mel West, University of Manchester
David Hopkins, Alma Harris and John Beresford, University of Nottingham
Geoff Southworth, University of Reading
July 2000

CHAPTER 1

Creating the Conditions for School Improvement

When we began teaching some 20 years or so ago 'change' was usually about working with new curriculum materials prepared by national or local agencies. Occasionally it may have meant trying out a new teaching strategy. In either case, most of these changes were *ad hoc*, self-determined, single innovations which by and large individual teachers decided to work on by themselves. More recently there has not been the luxury of choice. In this country as elsewhere, the change agenda has increasingly been set by national politicians, rather than educationalists. With the centralization of educational reform, teachers have seemingly lost control of change.

Our current work principally involves working with teachers and schools as they struggle, for the benefit of their students, to reassert control over the educational agenda. We are increasingly realizing that any change, be it externally or internally inspired, will be successful only to the extent that the school creates the conditions within which change and innovation can flourish. Ignoring this key insight accounts for the failure of so much educational reform. Irrespective of the myriad of policy initiatives that currently beset us, it is only teachers who are in the position to create good teaching. But even those teachers whose work is characterized by grace and fluidity, are only able to continue to grow in strong, supportive and collaborative school cultures. We consider ourselves fortunate that over the past few years we have learned a little about what are the most effective conditions for quality teaching and the ways of creating them. It is some of this experience that we share in this book.

Who is the Book For?

In writing this book we have had in mind the teachers, or indeed groups of teachers, who have assumed responsibility for development work in their schools. It may be the head or deputy, the appraisal or curriculum coordinator, the teacher in charge of staff development or of drawing up the school's development plan. It may even be those teachers who, although not part of the established hierarchy in the school, have a clear view of effective teaching and are taking on an informal leadership role within the school in order to share their vision with other colleagues. In short, this book is for anyone in a school who is taking responsibility for some form of development activity.

What Does the Book Do?

This book is not about what changes should be introduced into a school but rather about creating the conditions for supporting those changes which schools or individuals believe should be introduced. To be effective at managing change schools and teachers need to modify the internal conditions of the school *at the same time* as introducing changes in teaching or curriculum. The book therefore provides ideas and materials to help colleagues in school to create such conditions, and suggests a strategic approach.

How Should the Book be Used?

This book is not a step-by-step guide to school improvement. In our experience such 'quick-fix' approaches, although superficially attractive, rarely work in practice. Although schools can use similar broad approaches and strategies, there is no one way that is right for every school. Reinventing at least part of the wheel seems to be a necessary characteristic of successful school improvement. This book is therefore about recipes and ingredients rather than TV suppers. The book provides resources to be used within the context of the school's own aspirations. Consequently a key task of those using the suggestions and materials provided here will be to decide which of them are most suitable and for what purpose.

Chapters 3–8 consist of a series of materials that can be used to organize workshop activities in schools. These activities are intended to involve groups of staff in reviewing aspects of the school's conditions in order to support development activities. The materials include instructions for coordinators of such workshop activities, pages that might be used as overhead projector slides, and handouts that can be used to facilitate discussions.

How is the Book Organized?

As part of our work with schools we have identified six key conditions necessary for effective school improvement. The bulk of the book is taken up with describing in individual chapters what these conditions are, and in presenting staff development exercises on how they can he encouraged. Before this, in Chapter 2, we present a brief account of our current school improvement work and a rationale for the 'conditions' approach. At the end of the book we make some suggestions as to how a school can develop its own school improvement strategy. Some people may find it helpful to read the book cover to cover as an introduction to school improvement. Others, having a clear idea of where they are going, may wish just to plunder it for staff development activities. Both are fine by us – we hope that the book is organized sufficiently clearly to allow for both approaches, as well as those in between.

Where Do the Ideas Come From?

This book is based on our school improvement work which we have been pursuing in various guises and in different combinations of collaboration since the mid 1980s. Although we are for some of our life university teachers, we also work intensively with schools as facilitators of the change process. There are now some 100 schools in our network. As a consequence the book is grounded in practice, but also tested by reference to the available research evidence. Those who are interested in pursuing these ideas further should consult our *School Improvement in an Era of Change* (Hopkins *et al.*, 1994) which gives a more theoretical discussion of our approach, and provides many practitioner accounts of school-based work on the conditions for school improvements. We have also produced a companion volume to this book that focuses in a similarly practical way on what we regard as the other key component of school improvement. We called it *Creating the Conditions for Classroom Improvement* (Hopkins *et al.*, 1997).

It is appropriate however that this first handbook is about 'creating the conditions for school improvement'. Despite the abundance of policy initiatives and change efforts, too few of them, even the good ones, actually positively affect day-to-day life in classrooms. We hope that this little book will help in some way to get those useful and helpful changes behind the classroom door.

CHAPTER 2

Improving the Quality of Education for All

In the 1990s the educational agenda was increasingly being dominated by a concern to make sense of and implement the radical reform agenda of the late 1980s. This quest for stability however was being sought against a background of continuing change, as expectations for student achievement rose beyond the capacity of the system to deliver. It also became increasingly apparent that change and improvement are not necessarily synonymous. Although it is true that external pressure is often the cause, or at least the impetus, for most educational change, this is not to imply that such changes are always desirable. Indeed in our opinion, some externally imposed change should be resisted, or at least adapted to the school's own purpose.

As we work with schools within the framework of the national reform agenda we are committed to an approach to educational change that focuses on student achievement *and* the schools' ability to cope with change. We refer to this particular approach to educational change as *school improvement*. We regard school improvement as a distinct approach to educational change that enhances student outcomes *as well as* strengthening the school's capacity for managing change. In this sense school improvement is about raising student achievement through focusing on the teaching–learning process and the conditions which support it.

School improvement in the way that we define it is not, however, about how to implement centralized reforms in a more effective way. It is certainly not about blindly accepting the edicts of centralized policies, and striving to implement these directives uncritically. It is more to do with how schools can use the impetus of external reform to 'improve' or 'develop' themselves. Sometimes, what a school chooses to do in terms of school improvement will be consistent with the national reform agenda, at other times it will not. Whatever the case, the decision to engage in school improvement, at least in the schools that we work with, is based on clear evidence of what is the best for the young people in that school.

Since 1991 we have been working closely with some 100 schools in various parts of England and Wales, on a school improvement or development project known as Improving the Quality of Education for All (IQEA). This involves schools in working collaboratively with a group from the Institute of

Education at Cambridge and, latterly, at the University of Nottingham, and representatives from their Local Education Authority (LEA), or with a local support agency such as Bramley Grange College in Leeds. The overall aim of the project is to produce and evaluate a model of school development, and a programme of support, that strengthens a school's ability to provide quality education for all its pupils by building upon existing good practice. IQEA works from an assumption that schools are most likely to strengthen their ability to provide enhanced outcomes for all pupils when they adopt ways of working that are consistent with their own aspirations as well as the current reform agenda. At a time of great change in the educational system, the schools we are working with are using the impetus of external reform for internal purposes.

At the outset of IQEA we attempted to outline our vision of school improvement by articulating a set of principles that provided us with a philosophical and practical starting point. Because it is our assumption that schools are most likely to provide quality education and enhanced outcomes for pupils when they adopt ways of working that are consistent with these principles, they were offered as the basis for collaboration with those schools which wished to work with us. In short, we were inviting the schools to identify and to work on their own projects and priorities, but to do so in a way which embodied a set of 'core' values about school improvement. The principles represent both the expectation we have of the way project schools pursue school improvement, and as an *aide-mémoire* to ourselves. The five principles of IQEA are:

- The vision of the school (the school-in-the-future) should be one to which all members of the school community have an opportunity to contribute.
- The school will see in external pressures for change important opportunities to secure its internal priorities.
- The school will seek to create and maintain conditions in which all members of the school's community can learn successfully.
- The school will seek to adopt and develop structures which encourage collaboration and lead to the empowerment of individuals and groups.
- The school will seek to promote the view that the monitoring and evaluation of quality is a responsibility in which all members of staff share.

We feel that these principles have a synergism – together they are greater than the sum of their parts. They characterize an overall approach rather than prescribing a course of action. The intention is that they should inform the thinking and actions of teachers during school improvement efforts, and provide a touchstone for the strategies they devise and the behaviours they adopt.

We underpin our school improvement work with a *contract* between the partners in the project – the school and its teachers, in some cases, the LEA or sponsoring agency, and ourselves. The contract defines the parameters of the project and the obligations of those involved to each other. It is intended to clarify expectations and ensure the climate necessary for success. In particular the contract emphasizes that all staff be consulted, that coordinators are appointed, that a 'critical mass' of teachers are actively involved in development work, and that sufficient time is made available for classroom observation and staff development. For our part, we coordinate the project, provide training for the school coordinators and representatives, make regular school visits and contribute to staff training, provide staff development materials, and monitor the implementation of the project. The detail of the contract expresses in our opinion the minimum commitments necessary for success:

- The decision to participate in the project is made as a result of consultation amongst *all staff* in the school.
- Each school designates a minimum of four members of staff as project coordinators (one of whom is the head teacher) who attend training and support meetings (the group of coordinators is known as the 'project cadre').
- The whole school will allocate substantial staff development time to activities related to the project.
- At least 40 per cent of teachers (representing a cross section of staff) will take part in specified staff development activities in their own classrooms. Each participating teacher will be regularly 'released' from teaching in order to participate in these classroom-based aspects of the project.
- Each school will participate in the evaluation of the project and share findings with other participants in the project.

From the beginning of the project we were determined that we would attempt to affect all '*levels*' of the school. A major purpose of the contract is to ensure that this happens. One of the things that we had learned from research and our previous work is that change will not be successful unless it impacts all levels of the organization. Specifically our focus is on the three levels outlined in Figure 2.1 and the ways in which these interrelate. The *school level* is to do with overall management and the establishment of policies, particularly with respect to how resources and strategies for staff development can be mobilized to support school improvement efforts. At the level of *working groups* the concern is with working out the details of and arrangements for supporting improvement activities. Finally, at the *individual teacher* level the focus is on developing classroom practice.

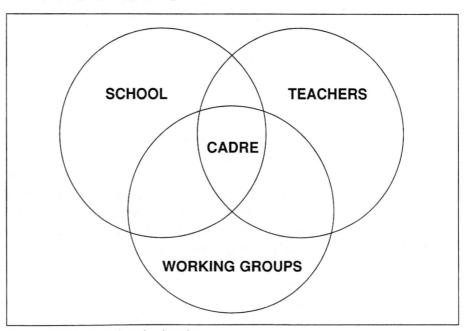

Figure 2.1 Integrating the levels

In very effective schools these three levels of activity are mutually support-ive. Consequently a specific aim of the IQEA project has to be to devise and establish positive conditions at each level and to coordinate support across these levels. It is in this connection that we require the establishment of a team of coordinators in each school whose task includes the integration of activities across the various levels. We refer to these coordinators, in associa-tion with advisory colleagues from the local authority, as *the cadre*. They are responsible for the day-to-day running of the project in their own school and for creating links between the ideas of the overall project and practical action. In many schools members of the cadre establish an *extended cadre* which serves to extend the project in a more formal way within the school.

So far we have summarized our broad approach to school improvement. There is now the conundrum of how best to support schools through this complex process. Our current thinking and practice is best summarized by describing what we do *within* and *outside* school.

Our *within* school work concerns the nature of our own intervention. As is by now quite obvious, we have explicitly chosen an interventionist role. Our roles vary from time to time and from place to place. On some occasions this may involve us in questioning our school-based colleagues in order to encour-age them to 'think aloud' about their work. Often they tell us that simply having an outsider who poses questions in a supportive way and then helps to set deadlines is in itself very helpful. However, having established a long-term agreement to collaborate with colleagues in a school, and then invested time in creating a working relationship with those colleagues, it is appropri-ate that we should be prepared to offer a critique of their proposals and actions. In this way we are seeking to balance our support with a degree of pressure that is intended to push their thinking forward.

It is important to add that we do at times elect to adopt more proactive roles in project schools. We do this in order to provide specific support to school coordinators at particular times. For example, we often contribute to school-based staff development programmes, working in partnership with school colleagues. Sometimes this involves us in team teaching in order to provide demonstrations, practice and feedback related to particular staff development techniques. We may also assist in the planning and processing of significant meetings. So, for example, one of us recently helped the head teacher and certain of his senior colleagues devise a plan for a key meeting of staff. This involved modelling how the meeting might be managed and then providing feedback as the head teacher and deputy head practised how they would carry out their tasks during the meeting.

Our *outside* school role focuses mainly on the meetings we hold for the various cohorts of schools involved in the project. There is a strong emphasis on 'reflection and enquiry' within these sessions. Reflection is the essential building block of professional competence and confidence. The training is based around the conditions we regard as necessary for successful school improvement which are described in detail in subsequent chapters of this book. Within training sessions we consistently try to model good staff devel-opment practice, share our knowledge of the change process, and provide time for high quality planning and consultancy. We also believe that it is appropriate that involvement of staff in school improvement should be acknowledged. Here an advantage of the school–university collaboration is

7

that it provides opportunities for teachers to accredit their school-based professional development activities through a series of academic awards.

Establishing a method of working with schools which was both flexible and focused was an issue which arose at the outset of IQEA. The method adopted in the project was to support each school in relation to its specific priority, while at the same time providing all schools with information about, and perspectives on, improvement strategies.

Keeping in mind this idea of a project made up of many individual school projects, we developed our own action framework. This framework (see Figure 2.2) provides the setting for a series of assumptions upon which the project is based. In describing these assumptions we relate them to the main components of the diagram, i.e. outcomes for students and staff; school culture; the school's background and organization; the selected developmental priorities; the conditions necessary to support such changes; and the school improvement strategy.

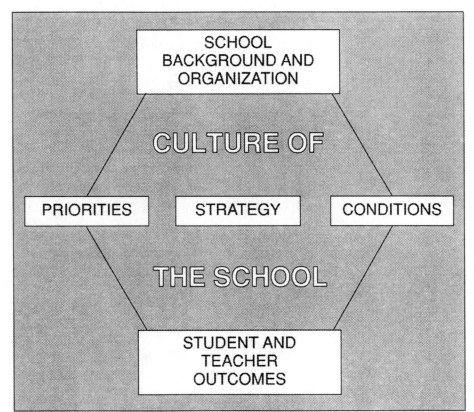

Figure 2.2 The 'logic' of school improvement

The first assumption is that school improvement will result in enhanced *outcomes* for students and staff. We define 'outcomes' broadly, and there will obviously be variations in outcome according to the focus of the improvement effort. For students, the outcomes could be critical thinking, learning capacity, self-esteem and so on, as well as improved examination and test results. For staff they could be increased collegiality, opportunities for professional learning and increased responsibility.

The second assumption is less obvious. School *culture* is the vital yet neglected dimension in the improvement process. It is, of course, a difficult concept to define. In general we see it as an amalgam of the values, norms and beliefs that characterize the way in which a group of people behave within a specific organizational setting. The types of school cultures most supportive of school improvement efforts, and those that we are working towards in IQEA, are those that are collaborative, have high expectations for both students and staff, exhibit a consensus on values (or an ability to deal effectively with differences), and support an orderly and secure environment.

The third assumption is that the school's *background and organization* are key factors in the school improvement process. Unfortunately most school improvement efforts address organizational factors, which are often the main inhibitors of change, as only explanatory factors. It is also interesting to note that a school's organizational structure is inevitably a reflection of its values. Consequently, there is a strong, but not clearly understood, relationship between the school's organization and its culture.

The fourth assumption is that school improvement works best when there is a clear and practical focus for the development effort. The school's *priorities* are normally some aspect of curriculum, assessment or classroom process which the school has identified from the many changes that confront it. In this sense, the choice represents the school's interpretation of the current reform agenda. Although the balance of activities varies from school to school, we find that more successful schools set priorities for development that:

- are few in number – trying to do too much is counter-productive
- are central to the mission of the school
- relate to the current reform agenda
- link to teaching and learning
- lead to specific outcomes for students and staff.

The fifth assumption is that the *conditions* for school improvement are worked on at the same time as the curriculum or other priorities the school has set itself. Conditions are the internal features of a school and ways of working that enable it to get work done. Without an equal focus on conditions, even priorities that meet the above criteria can quickly become marginalized. We have also found that when circumstances exist that are less supportive of change, it is necessary in the initial stages to concentrate much more on creating the internal conditions within the school which facilitate development, limiting work on the priorities until the conditions are in place. It is the creation of these conditions for school improvement that provide the focus for this book.

The sixth assumption is that a school improvement *strategy* needs to be developed in order to link priorities to the conditions. The strategy will need to be more or less powerful depending on the relative 'strength' of the other factors. Strategies take very different forms. In many cases, however, a school will use the opportunity of an external change (and the additional resources that often go with it) as a means of linking a priority for development to the necessary conditions. For example, many schools are using teacher appraisal as a strategy for linking together work on teaching styles (priority) with peer observation in the classroom (condition).

This framework for school improvement is based on our belief that effective change strategies focus not only on the implementation of centralized policies or chosen initiatives, but also on creating the conditions within schools that can sustain the teaching–learning process. In our experience unless this is the case then the impact of any change will only be tangential to the daily life of the school. The most successful schools increase their capacity to handle change by linking together priorities and conditions in imaginative and innovative ways.

From our work on the IQEA project, we have been able to elaborate a series of conditions that underpin the work of these successful schools. Taken together they result in the creation of opportunities for teachers to feel more powerful and confident about their work. This is particularly important because difficulties often occur for both individual teachers and the school when development work begins. Teachers, for example, may be faced with acquiring new teaching skills or with mastering new curriculum material. The school as a consequence may be forced into new ways of working that are incompatible with existing organizational structures. This phase of 'destabilization' or 'internal turbulence' is as predictable as it is uncomfortable. Yet many research studies have found that without a period of destabilization successful, long-lasting change is unlikely to occur.

The schools that we work with survive periods of instability by either consciously or intuitively adapting or accommodating their *internal conditions* to meet the demands of the change. As we discuss in Chapter 9 we encourage schools to diagnose their internal conditions in relation to their chosen change before they begin developmental work. They can then begin to build these modifications into the strategies they are going to adopt. Although the following list represents our best estimate (rather than a definitive statement) of what the important conditions are at present, we believe that there is both research based and practical evidence to support them. Broadly stated the conditions are:

- Proper attention to the potential benefits of *enquiry and reflection.*
- A commitment to *collaborative planning.*
- The *involvement* of staff, students and the community in school policies and decisions.
- A commitment to *staff development.*
- Effective *coordination* strategies.
- Effective *leadership*, but not just of the head; the leadership function is spread throughout the school.

In the following chapters we provide materials and activities that we find useful when trying to help schools to review and develop these six conditions.

CHAPTER 3

Enquiry and Reflection

We have observed that those schools which recognize that enquiry and reflection are important processes in school improvement find it easier to sustain improvement effort around established priorities, and are better placed to monitor the extent to which policies actually deliver the intended outcomes for pupils. Central to the conditions which promote the effective use of enquiry and reflection as developmental tools are:

3.1 Systematic collection, interpretation and use of school-generated data in decision making.
3.2 Effective strategies for reviewing the progress and impact of school policies and initiatives.
3.3 Widespread involvement of staff in the processes of data collection and analysis.
3.4 Clear ground rules for the collection, control and use of school-based data.

Enquiry and Reflection: Overview

Whether initiated externally to facilitate judgements about a school's performance (e.g., inspection), or internally to review the progress of policies or programmes (e.g., curriculum mapping), we have found that schools are increasingly interested in the generation of information which can be used to assess how the school is 'working'. One of the ironies we associate with this interest is the fact that information gathered by outsiders, be they inspectors or consultants, is often seen as having more significance than information which is routinely available to those within the school community. Further, we have observed that where schools understand the potential of internally generated information about progress or difficulties, they are better placed to exploit opportunities and to overcome problems.

We believe, therefore, that in a large number of schools the range of data available is being underused. Instead of being brought to bear on decisions confronting the school, or being used to increase understanding of present strengths and weaknesses, information is overlooked, and uncoordinated. A

11

further irony is that often considerable effort has been put into the amassing of such information, as we frequently record, report or file pieces of information despite there being little prospect of purposeful use.

Of course, some schools are much better organized in this area, and have clear systems and procedures for collecting, analysing and interpreting information which is seen as relevant to particular aspects of the school or particular decisions. Even in these cases, however, a more general commitment to enquire into and reflect on the school's progress is rare – more often it is the issue that is identified then the information collected, rather than data being collected to help identify what the issue should be.

We would not want to suggest here that everything which takes place in a school can be noted, nor that all information has equal significance. But our work with schools that have adopted a sustained commitment to improvement initiatives has led us to identify the habits of enquiry and reflection as important forces for improvement. Indeed, we believe that this condition underpins the quality of efforts in the other conditions outlined in this book.

This chapter offers some ideas and activities to help the school to review its efforts in this area. It builds on our experience that it is often better to start with a limited and clearly focused enquiry. This seems sensible both because the large-scale audit activities which have been associated with development planning can produce so much information that staff are overwhelmed rather than enlightened, and because, in keeping with our notion of 'building capacity' within the school, a carefully planned, small-scale enquiry is a useful way to develop enquiry skills amongst the staff group which can subsequently be coordinated around larger projects.

The activities themselves, whilst in no sense constituting a comprehensive vehicle for school review, have been selected to highlight those features of the enquiry and reflection process which have emerged from our own work with schools. They relate to the key ingredients of an effective policy for collecting and using school-generated data to promote school improvement. These are:

- adopting a systematic approach to information collection and interpretation activities
- ensuring that information about the impact of policies and programmes is available to help assess the links between policy and practice
- involving *all staff* in procedures for information collection and analysis
- ensuring that there are appropriate safeguards so that confidential or sensitive information is properly handled.

Activity 3.1: Systematic Collection and Interpretation of Data

Context

The amount of information available within schools, but not often considered in any organized way, is to some extent a result of the time pressure under which most teachers work. Nevertheless, it offers a rich vein of data about the way the school is functioning which we need to tap into if we are to develop understanding of the school's processes and effects.

One of the major sources of information about how the school is functioning is the pupils. Though all teachers are inevitably aware of some pupil feelings and responses, few schools have established systems for collecting and analysing pupil views on a regular basis. Often our awareness of what it feels like to be a pupil in our own school is restricted to what we observe in our own lessons and what we pick up around the school. One way of improving our understanding of the quality of experience the school makes available is to spend a day as a 'pupil', trying to look at the school through a pupil's eyes. This activity offers some ideas about how such an enquiry might be structured. It is important to involve as many staff as possible in this activity.

Briefing

Aims

- To give teachers some flavour of what it feels like to be a pupil in the school. In so doing, to provide teachers with 'information' about the way the school operates which is not usually available to them.

- To offer a structure in which teachers can reflect on the usefulness and problems associated with gathering such information.

Process

The activity is structured in five steps. Steps 1 and 2, which relate to the expectation and beliefs we hold about pupil experience, involve individual reflection and discussion with a colleague. These can be organized to take place during a staff INSET session or could be carried out by pairs of staff at convenient times. Step 3 involves planning and carrying out a pupil tracking exercise. This obviously will need to be planned for in each individual case, and where a number of staff are involved, may need to be spread out over a number of days or weeks. Steps 4 and 5 can only be carried out after a group of staff has completed Step 3, and are suitable for a staff meeting or INSET session at which all those involved can come together.

Step 1   Individually, list the range of opportunities and experiences that you would hope are made available to each pupil during a 'typical' day in the school. You may find it helpful to distinguish between the range of learning opportunities provided, and the balance of topics or subjects through which these are provided. You may also feel it is useful to identify your expectations regarding pupils' use of equipment/resources in practical subjects.

- Range of learning opportunities

- Range of topics/subjects

- Access to/use of resources

© IQEA – Creating the Conditions for School Improvement

Step 2   Join with a colleague and compare your lists. Try to agree on *three* opportunities/experiences which you believe should be made available to all pupils during each day.

We believe that all pupils should have access to the following opportunities/experiences each day:

1.

2.

3.

Step 3   **Planning pupil tracking**

Identify a pupil or pupil group whose experience you would like to tap into, and arrange to follow that pupil/group, ideally through a whole day at the school (where this is not possible, it may be possible to arrange to spend part of a day or parts of different days carrying out this activity). Remember that this will need to be negotiated with the colleagues whose lessons you will need to attend. In negotiating with colleagues you should stress that:

- the pupil's experience and response is the focus

- no judgements about the teacher will be made on the basis of this activity

- it is important that lessons are conducted in as 'normal' a fashion as possible.

| Step 4 | **Debriefing the tracking exercise** |

Following the tracking exercise, meet with colleagues who have also carried out the activity and discuss the following questions.

- What picture of the pupil's day is emerging from our experience?

- How widely are the experiences/opportunities we see as important being made available to pupils in a routine day at the school?

- What (if anything) have we learned from this experience which surprises us?

- What might we do to improve the range and quality of pupil experience?

| Step 5 | **Debriefing the activity** |

Reflecting on this exercise, consider:

- How important/useful is this kind of information in planning for school improvement?

- How important is it to establish that each member of staff can contribute to the overall picture?

- Are there other aspects of school life where we could usefully build up a more systematic picture of what is happening?

- How can systematic enquiry of this sort be built into our normal information processing and decision-making procedures?

Activity 3.2: Monitoring Policies in Practice

Context

It is not always easy to identify how far the agreed policies of the school are actually carried forward into classroom practice. Indeed, there seems to have been a significant increase during recent years in the number and quality of policies schools publish. Whether or not these have the intended impact is less clear. This is not because data are not available, but because they are spread among many colleagues, all of whom only see part of the overall picture. Further emphasis on the need for schools to 'know' what is happening in terms of policy implementation has been provided by the procedures for school inspection.

This activity provides an opportunity for staff to consider what mechanisms currently exist to monitor classroom practice, and to evaluate the effectiveness of these mechanisms. It is focused around the lists of criteria and related evidence on teaching quality drawn up by OFSTED and used in the inspection process.

Briefing

Aims

- To give staff an opportunity to evaluate the effectiveness of current methods for monitoring classroom practice.

- To build from this to a more general discussion of the ways information is/could be used to enhance knowledge of the school's performance.

Process

This activity is structured in five steps, and has been organized so that it could be carried out during a professional development day or in a staff development session.

Step 1 involves individual reflection, and could be carried out individually before the day/session as a preparation activity; Step 2 requires colleagues to work together in twos or threes, sharing their thoughts. Step 3 is a whole-group activity, which should be carried out either as a single staff group or (if the staff is too large for a meaningful single discussion group) in smaller groupings which are then brought together to pool their findings. Step 4 is again an individual activity based on the whole-group discussion, which may then be debriefed in the final plenary stage (Step 5).

Step 1   Individually, consider the following list of criteria and decide how far you are able to agree with this list. What would you want to add to it in order to be 'satisfied' that you have an acceptable set of criteria relating to quality of teaching?

Pair with a colleague and compare your responses.

Evaluation Criteria

Teaching quality is to be judged by the extent to which:

- teachers have clear objectives for their lessons;
- pupils are aware of these objectives;
- teachers have a secure command of the subject;
- lessons have suitable content;
- activities are well chosen to promote learning of that content;
- activities are presented in ways which will engage, motivate and challenge all pupils, enabling them to make progress at a suitable pace.

<u>Additions:</u>

© *IQEA – Creating the Conditions for School Improvement*

Step 2   Remaining in pairs, compile a list of possible sources of evidence of the school's performance in these areas. Compare your list with the suggested range of sources of evidence identified in the guidelines for school inspection, given in the box below.

Sources of Evidence

- planning of work: forecasts, lesson plans and individual notes;
- lesson observation;
- discussion with teachers and pupils;
- samples of pupils' work, including homework;
- marking, comments and follow-up;
- teachers' records of work done by pupils;
- the nature and contribution of homework;
- role(s) of classroom assistants;
- input from specialist teachers;
- individual education plans for pupils with statements of special educational needs.

Step 3   As a whole group, list those procedures that you currently use in the school to monitor the quality of teaching.

- What are the criteria used?

- What sources of 'evidence' are regularly drawn on?

- Who gathers/interprets the 'evidence'?

- What use is made of the findings?

Step 4

Individually, list three ways *you* could improve your own use of evidence to assess the quality of your own teaching:

1.

2.

3.

Step 5

As a whole group, share your ideas for improving the evidence available to assess the quality of teaching in the school. List any ideas you feel should be followed up by yourself or others at a later stage.

Activity 3.3: Involving Staff in Data Collection and Analysis Activities

Context

We have suggested that all staff have a role to play in the collection and analysis of data relevant to the assessment of school performance and the decisions schools need to make. A particularly fertile area for investigation is the classroom. Indeed, willingness to explore classroom practice and share the findings with colleagues has been a common feature of those schools we have been working alongside on improvement projects. This activity provides a format for paired observation, that is, the pairing of teachers who undertake to observe one another in a classroom setting and offer feedback.

Although Step 1 is not essential, we would recommend that it is undertaken as a preparatory activity, preferably on a whole-school or departmental basis. It is also important to remember that this activity will probably take place over a number of weeks, and may need to be 'monitored' by someone in the school to ensure progress is maintained.

Briefing

Aims

- To underline the view that *all* teachers are important sources of information and feedback.

- To provide an opportunity for colleagues to share one another's classroom practice.

Process

This activity takes place in three separate stages. Step 1, which is designed to raise awareness of the range of views and approaches which exist among colleagues, should be carried out before the paired observation (Step 2) is organized. Step 2 is likely to be individually planned and to take several weeks to complete if a number of colleagues join in. Step 3 involves bringing together those who have participated to discuss their experiences. A sensible time-scale for the whole process is probably a half-term period, with Step 1 early, Step 3 towards the end, and a five or six week period in between when Step 2 can be individually negotiated between pairings.

Reflection on Teaching

Activity sequence

1. On your own consider the *matrix* below. It was devised by a group of teachers who were asked to list ways in which they *cater for individuals* in their classrooms.
2. Put in the empty boxes any strategies that you use in addition to the ones listed. Having done this put an asterisk alongside the *three* strategies that you think are most powerful.
3. Join up with three other people and compare your results. Discuss similarities and differences.
4. Choose one strategy and share ideas as to how it can be used. Present your conclusions to the other groups.

Evaluation

1. What aspects of your teaching could be developed?
2. How might you go about a process of development?

Discussion Material

Classroom Strategies Chart

SETTING INDIVIDUAL TASKS		TALKING TO INDIVIDUALS
	GIVING PUPILS CHOICE	PRAISING CHILDREN'S EFFORT
GETTING TO KNOW PARENTS	VARIED MATERIALS	SMALL GROUP WORK
	LISTENING TO INDIVIDUALS	RECORDING PROGRESS

Step 2   **Organizing paired observation**

Paired observation involves teachers acting as a 'mirror' to a colleague, reflecting back to him/her their own classroom practice. Experience suggests that such observation is most useful when it is clearly focused, conducted according to agreed criteria, and the feedback is non-judgemental. When planning paired observation the following stages may prove useful.

- **Select pairings.**
  These need to reflect the purpose of observation and involve colleagues who are comfortable with one another.

- **Arrange a pre-observation planning meeting.**
  At this meeting it is important to identify the focus of the observation, those aspects of classroom practice which need to be recorded to shed light on the focus (i.e., what do we count as evidence?) and how the information will be recorded.

- **'Timetable' the observation.**
  The particular lesson to be observed needs to be agreed in advance and to reflect the focus.

- **Carry out post-observation feedback.**
  This needs to take place as soon as possible after the observation. It should provide an opportunity for both partners to 'make sense' of the experience, and for the observer to help the teacher to consider what developments (if any) in practice he/she might target.

- **Reverse roles and repeat.**

Step 3   **Debriefing**

Where a number of teachers have been engaging in paired observation, there are often general issues arising which it is worth discussing as a staff group. Of course, this needs to be done in a way which does not compromise the confidentiality of the encounter. It should therefore focus on the processes and values of observation, not the aspects of the teachers' practice selected for observation. The following questions may prove useful in stimulating a discussion amongst teachers who have participated.

- What have we learned from one another as a result of paired observation?

- What have we learned about acting as an observer to a colleague?

- What would we do differently if we were to repeat this exercise in the future?

- Are there ways we can use this experience in the wider context of staff development within the school?

© *IQEA – Creating the Conditions for School Improvement*

Context

Collecting information in schools inevitably involves other people, their behaviour and their points of view. It is important therefore to consider the ethical implications of any process of inquiry. As a matter of principle it is vital that the individual rights of those involved should be protected, whether they are colleagues, pupils or parents. On a more pragmatic level, the future of any development will depend upon the goodwill of everybody involved.

Arguably the key ethical issues to bear in mind relate to confidentiality, negotiation and control. Confidential information should not be released until it has been agreed with the person or persons to whom it belongs. In carrying out some form of inquiry, therefore, it is wise to establish some form of ground rules that address these issues.

Briefing

Aims

- To remind staff that enquiry often involves the sharing of sensitive or confidential information.

- To help colleagues to draw up a 'Code of Ethics' which can be used as reference point for school-based enquiry.

Process

This activity builds from individual anxieties and concerns toward a set of 'ground rules' for information collection and use. Step 1 involves individuals working alone, Steps 2 and 3 are conducted as a whole staff group.

The nature of the topic under discussion implies that there will need to be effective management of Steps 2 and 3 if a usable document is to emerge. There should therefore be a clearly designated leader to take the staff through these stages of the activity.

Make a list of the rules you would like to see applied, bearing in mind the ideas 'confidentiality, negotiation and control'. Number your list in order of importance.

Step 2

The group leader takes the first item from each person and records it on a large sheet or OHP. When all participants have provided one item they may offer any additional items to make up the list.

Step 3

The group discusses the list and agrees a set of ground rules. These may need to be kept under review.

CHAPTER 4

Planning

Our experience, alongside that of colleagues in many schools, tells us that planning for development is an essential part of the school improvement process. Planning is enriched when staff draw upon the data produced by enquiry and reflection activities (see Chapter 3). Also, the process of planning should involve as many members of staff and other groups (e.g., governors) as possible. However, there is one danger to avoid in devising priorities and plans: do not regard your plan as entirely fixed – plans need to be flexible not rigid.

4.1 There need to be strong links between the school's vision and plans for improvement.

4.2 The process of planning is as important as having a plan.

4.3 Plans need to be known by all involved.

4.4 Plans need to be constantly updated and modified.

Planning: Overview

The quality of school-level planning is a central factor in enabling the school to develop. All who are involved in the improvement of the school need to have a sense of direction for the journeys they are embarked upon. With the widespread use of school development plans there are probably few who would disagree with the need for plans. However, our experience also suggests that some staff are less aware of the need to address four particular aspects of planning.

First, plans for improving the school must be strongly linked to the school's vision. The beliefs and values which the school promotes and pursues must be congruent with the initiatives and innovations which are being adopted and implemented. The core mission of the school must be explicitly related to plans for development. Then the school can grow in ways which are compatible with the school's values, and any changes which are adopted will develop practice and simultaneously strengthen educational beliefs.

Second, the process of planning is at least as important as having a plan. Some of us would agree that what is really essential is planning, not plans.

Others might say that the plan should be a by-product of the planning process. Whatever emphasis you adopt the message is clear: the means by which plans are produced are absolutely vital. It is imperative that staff are involved, differences shared and action steps identified and agreed. This latter point is especially significant. A development plan needs to move into action. Plans should be judged not in terms of their articulation of destinations to be reached, but rather, in terms of how they are leading to action. Plans and planning should make things happen.

Third, plans need to be known by all who are involved with the development project. In part, this point relates to the second. If the process of planning is collaborative and participative then you and your colleagues will know what is going on as well as why and how. Moreover, it is important to consider others outside the school and what they will need to know. Plans should be communicated to everyone who has a stake in the school.

If communication is important, so too is it necessary to keep everyone aware of progress being made. Not only do you and your colleagues need to know what the plan is, but also how well you are doing in working towards the agreed goal. For this reason progress checks will be needed to enable you to gauge the pace of implementation and the success of the plan.

Fourth, experience tells us that no plan is able to anticipate all eventualities at the outset. As progress checks are conducted then adjustments will be needed to ensure you keep making headway. The plan will need updating to keep it in tune with the present – if not, the plan will become outdated and irrelevant. In this sense, you need to keep the plan evolving. Hence, planning is a constant process, not a one-off event to get started. Planning keeps the improvement process going. Planning therefore needs to be a process which involves many staff, keeps everyone informed of intentions and actions and is on-going, because initial ideas need to be reshaped in the light of new circumstances. Re-planning will keep you and the school moving forward.

Activity 4.1: Linking Visions and Planning

Context

Often in schools the need to deal with the immediate means that planning engages with short-term purposes. Improvement initiatives however have to be seen as being long-term if they can be successful. The process of planning and the plan need to connect to the vision of the school in order to help transport those hopes into actions and to ensure that the actions are consistent with the vision.

Briefing

Aims

- To consider the long-term goals for the school and then to work backwards from them to begin to determine how you will move from where you are to where you want to be.

Process

The activity is organized into three steps. At each step participants need sufficient time to explore, clarify and agree on the goals and actions needed. All three steps could take place during an INSET session (say a half or even whole day). Alternatively, the steps could be staged over a series of meetings – Step 1 could be completed at one meeting, Step 2 at the next.

Encourage participants to be detailed and concrete when thinking about the actions the school takes. Use flipchart paper to record decisions and outcomes at each step.

At the end of Step 3 put the summary sheets (flipchart papers) together and see if a clear route forward from Step 3 to Step 1 has developed. If not encourage participants to make these connections between the steps.

Back to the Future

This is a procedure to help groups of staff to work creatively in developing plans that will help move the school towards its development goals. Discussion moves through a series of steps.

Step 1

> What is the goal the group is trying to achieve? Imagine you are at the time in the future when this has been achieved. Describe what you will see happening.

Step 2

> Now look back. How did you get to this position? What steps occurred that allowed the school to achieve its goal? Consider alternative routes. Remember to talk in the past tense.

Step 3

> In the light of these discussions agree the best way of making the journey to the future you have in mind. Now you can talk about what you intend to do.

Context

One common weakness with development plans is that once they have been created, little attention is devoted to putting the plan into action. We are convinced from our experience that having drawn up the development plan staff next need to devise an action plan to ensure that the plan is implemented.

Moreover, the process of planning the implementation phase should enable staff to feel they know what is happening and what they need to do. The process of action planning should help staff to move easily from planning into action.

Briefing

Aims

- To focus attention on the need to devise action plans which will make the agreed priorities happen.

- To develop success criteria for an agreed priority.

- To develop a process of action planning which is collaborative and helps colleagues know what is happening and who is responsible for which tasks.

Process

The activity comprises four steps. Each step builds on the previous one. If groups undertake this activity, membership of the groups needs to remain constant. Step 1 is a relatively straightforward and quick stage to complete. Steps 2, 3 and 4 will take longer. Step 2 can prove difficult but is central to the whole activity. Allow participants plenty of time to complete this step. Encourage them to be as explicit as possible about the success criteria. Vague criteria are not very helpful.

Step 3 should involve participants naming specific colleagues. Ensure senior staff are named as well as other members of staff. These names should appear in Step 4.

The activity could take place over a number of sessions spaced out by days or over several weeks.

Step 1

Identify the particular development you plan to implement. Briefly list the key objectives:

Step 2

How will you recognize whether the development priority has been successful and the objective met? List any criteria or measures you can use to indicate success:

Step 3

Think about the people who will be involved in carrying through, or will be affected by the development work. Think in particular about what they need to know, what they need to feel and what they need to do if the change is to be successful. List these:

i)   They will need to develop knowledge/understanding of...

ii) They will need to develop positive attitudes towards/about...

iii) They will need to develop the skills necessary to be able to...

Step 4

Taking the lists of knowledge, attitudes, and skills identified, place these in rank order according to how influential you believe each will be in successfully implementing the change. Then consider how to bring each objective about: What action is required? By whom? What resources will be involved? What success criteria have been identified? When will the work be completed?
(See Appendix page 128 for full-page master of this form.)

Objective	Action Required	By Whom?	Resources Required	Success Criteria	Complete by

Context

Having invested time and energy in plans and planning, it is sensible to check from time to time how the plans are proceeding. Indeed, it is important to check whether the plan is being implemented. This activity helps you to introduce progress checks and to use success criteria and performance indicators to gauge how far you have travelled and what else needs to be done.

Briefing

Aims

- To promote the idea of progress checks.

- To encourage the use of success criteria to gauge progress and implementation.

- To focus attention on the extent to which progress checks are currently used in the school.

Process

This activity is a mix of general discussion and focused tasks. There are three steps. Step 1 is based around two OHTs. This step could be conducted as a plenary session. It is useful to encourage general discussion of each point on the two OHTs.

Step 2 focuses on OHT 3. This could be discussed in plenary, or used as a starter for working in groups.

Step 3 asks participants to try out the ideas from OHTs 1, 2 and 3. This step is concerned with the practical application of the points discussed in Steps 1 and 2. Step 3 will take longer than Steps 1 and 2, somewhere between one and two hours depending upon the size of the group and the depth of detail required.

At the end of Step 3 review how participants now feel about progress checks, success criteria and the use of them in your school.

This activity invites you to consider the idea of progress checks and to examine the extent to which they are currently used in your school's planning.

Step 1

Show OHTs of the statements below and invite colleagues to discuss the idea of progress checks. OHTs 1 and 2 are taken from *Planning for School Development* (DES, 1989).

OHT 1
(See Appendix p. 129 for OHT master.)

> **Regular progress checks involve:**
>
> - giving somebody in the team responsibility for ensuring that the progress checks take place
> - reviewing progress at team meetings, especially when taking the next step forward or making decisions about future directions
> - deciding what will count as evidence of progress in relation to the success criteria
> - finding quick methods of collecting evidence from different sources
> - recording the evidence and conclusions for later use.

OHT 2
(See Appendix p. 130 for OHT master.)

> **Some progress checks may show that:**
>
> - the time schedules were too tight
> - circumstances have changed since the plan was constructed and unexpected obstacles have been encountered
> - there is a loss of direction and some mid-course correction is required for the target to be met.

Step 2

Progress checks are made easier when SUCCESS CRITERIA have been established and communicated to all involved in a project. Consider the following points about success criteria (either produce a copy for everyone or make into an OHT). What does the group think about success criteria? OHT 3 is taken from *The Empowered School* (Hargreaves and Hopkins, 1991).

OHT 3
(See Appendix p. 131 for OHT master.)

> **Success Criteria**
>
> *Success criteria* are a form of school-generated performance indicator which:
> - give *clarity* about the target: what exactly are you trying to achieve?
> - point to the *standard* expected by the team
> - provide advance warning of the *evidence* needed to judge successful implementation
> - give an indication of the *time-scale* involved.

1. Identify a priority in the school's development plan (different groups or colleagues might choose different priorities, or you could all focus on the same one). Either generate success criteria for this priority or, if success criteria have been established, review them in the light of Step 2.

2. Now conduct a progress check on this priority area.

3. Share your findings from 2 with your colleagues.

4. Decide upon what action is needed to continue and sustain work in this priority area.

    By whom?

    When by?

5. How will this be incorporated into your existing plans?

Context

One of the aspects of planning which we have found interesting is the fact that while schools can experience difficulty in putting together meaningful plans, simultaneously they display a reluctance to modify these plans, despite their shortcomings. Staff often comment to us that they dislike the plans they have made, yet they do nothing to change them!

Moreover, many schools tend to favour a cycle of planning which becomes enshrined in the school year. Planning is therefore fixed to occur at set points in the year. Consequently, this means there are times of the year when staff are planning intensively, while at other times no planning is taking place at all. Therefore, there are occasions when issues arise, or initiatives arrive, and it is very difficult for the school to respond.

This activity asks you to review your school's capacity to meet changing priorities.

Briefing

Aims

- To draw attention to the need for schools to retain a capacity to respond to initiatives.

- To consider how flexible your school's existing planning processes actually are.

Process

Work in quite small groups if possible – threes and fours would be ideal.

There are three steps to follow. Step 1 presents the scenario. Participants should focus on questions 1 and 2. Encourage full answers and reasons. Invite colleagues to record their responses.

Step 2 is a plenary activity. After the presentations spend time identifying any emerging issues.

Step 3 is an important part of the activity and time needs to be reserved for this. Do Step 3 in small groups, and finish with a plenary session to share outcomes.

Step 1

Consider the following scenario and then in small groups address questions 1 and 2.

Your school has learned that there is an opportunity to take part in a major National Curriculum project. Participation in the project will bring with it an injection of many thousands of pounds into the school's budget.

To be considered for the project a comprehensive bid must be made by a group of staff within the next fortnight of term time.

Q.1 What do you think your school *would* do?

Q.2 What do you believe the school *should* do to be eligible?

Step 2

Allow the small groups to share their predictions. When all have presented, search for similarities and group them.

Are there any issues emerging from the reports? What are they? Discuss them.

Emerging issues are:

Step 3

In the light of issues identified in Step 2, what have you learned about your school's capacity to respond to initiatives?

Can you formulate a proposal for ensuring the school develops a capacity to respond?

What are the implications of this activity for the planning cycles in your school?

CHAPTER 5

Involvement

Successful schools seem to have ways of working that encourage feelings of involvement. This provides support for the school's efforts as well as a range of additional resources that can be used to enhance learning opportunities. It also creates a strong sense of community identity that encourages a commitment to achieving high standards. In this chapter we examine the following ideas:

5.1 The school should have policies for encouraging involvement of pupils, staff, parents, governors and community.
5.2 Participation has to be encouraged by procedures.
5.3 Access needs to be facilitated by the creation of an open climate.
5.4 The involvement of external support agencies has to be planned carefully.

In the research literature on effective schools there is strong evidence that success is associated with a sense of identity and involvement among pupils, staff, parents and the wider community. Indeed the picture that emerges is one of a well-integrated community within which all those involved have a high sense of commitment to the school's success. One researcher has referred to what he calls 'an incorporative approach' whereby successful schools establish patterns of working that foster feelings of involvement.

Our own experience certainly supports this line of argument, suggesting that schools need to develop strategies that encourage the involvement of pupils, staff (not just teachers), parents, governors, external support agencies and members of the community at large. When these groups feel isolated from what the school is trying to achieve there is a strong likelihood that they can become obstacles to progress. For example, the capacity of pupils to act as barriers to innovation is frequently underestimated. While they may not stand up and actively oppose proposed changes in the school's ways of working, their responses can be determined forces of resistance. Despite this it is not uncommon to find that schools do not even alert pupils to changes that are being introduced.

Pupil involvement does seem to be a particularly important factor in school improvement. This can occur at a routine organizational level, by involving them in decision making and encouraging them to take some responsibility for day-to-day routines. We have also come across some excellent examples of pupils being seen as a source of active support in improvement initiatives. For example, some schools have invited pupils to participate in staff development activities in order that teachers can gain a better understanding of the perspective of the learner. Certainly at the very least it is important to seek pupil feedback on their reactions to innovations that are introduced.

Arguably the most important dimension to pupil involvement occurs at the classroom level, where they can be encouraged to take responsibility for their own learning. This can also facilitate their learning of organizational, planning, discussion, decision making and leadership skills. All of this assumes, of course, that schools are places where children and adults are skilful in working together, sharing their ideas and supporting one another. It also assumes that there are two major resources for learning available in the classroom: the teacher and the pupils. Consequently teachers have to be skilful in organizing their classes in ways that encourage cooperation.

The incorporative approach can be extended beyond the school gate to include parents and, indeed, members of the local community including, of course, governors. Here the attitudes of staff are vital. If they see such groups as a potential hindrance to their work they are unlikely to encourage their participation. On the other hand if they see members of the wider community as sources of potential help, they are much more likely to generate relationships that will encourage participation.

A further dimension relates to the involvement of external agencies as a support to staff in extending their responses to pupils. Our experience is that some schools are particularly enterprising in drawing on the resources of such people. This enterprise includes being skilful in knowing how best to utilize outsiders in ways that make effective use of their expertise and time.

The materials and activities in the rest of this chapter will help you and your colleagues to review and, possibly, develop policy and practices in order to make better use of all members of the school community. Specifically the focus will be on:

- policies for encouraging involvement
- procedures that facilitate participation
- the creation of an open climate
- the effectiveness of external support agencies.

Activity 5.1: Policies for Involvement

Context

Why is involvement so important?

It seems from research that very successful schools encourage everybody to get involved in supporting their work. Schools can be seen as small communities consisting of people with different points of view and expectations. The aim should be to encourage everybody to pull broadly in the same direction. The assumption is that the school will be more effective in achieving its goals when everybody feels involved in and committed to broadly the same purposes. These materials will help you and your colleagues to review the levels of involvement that exist at present and, perhaps, to pinpoint some areas for development.

Briefing

Aims

- To provide staff with an opportunity to analyse existing policies for involving staff, pupils, governors, parents and other members of the community.

- To look specifically at how school documentation might be improved in order to encourage involvement.

Process

Following a general introduction to the topic, Step 1 involves individuals in reflecting upon and making notes about the school's existing policies. If there is time it would be helpful to invite pairs of colleagues to compare their ideas before moving on to the next step. Step 2 focuses particular attention on a range of school documents. Group sizes of four or five would be most appropriate here. It might be that different groups address different types of documents. Step 3 involves members of the groups in recording their analysis on the form that is provided.

Finally, Step 4 widens the discussion to a consideration of overall school policy in the light of the analysis of the documents. It might conclude with discussion of actions to be taken.

Step 1   Before we discuss the issue of involvement in detail, make some notes about the school's policies for involving:

- Staff

- Pupils

- Governors

- Parents

- Community

Step 2   Divide into working groups. Each group examines one recent school document that addresses one of the groups in the school community. Examples might be:

- Schemes of work
- Worksheet
- Discipline codes/school rules
- Governors' report

- Letters to parents
- Option choice forms
- School brochures
- Prospectus

Step 3   As a group consider the following questions with respect to the document you have examined. Make notes of your own views during the discussion.

Who is the audience?

Who seems to have been the author?

If you were the intended audience what impression would the document give?

How might the document be improved?

Step 4   Present your group findings to the other groups. Discuss the following questions:

- Are these documents encouraging involvement?
- How might they be improved?
- What does this suggest about current school policies?
- What have you learned from this exercise?

© *IQEA – Creating the Conditions for School Improvement*

Activity 5.2: Encouraging Involvement

Context

Schools are complex social organizations. They vary in terms of the extent to which the various stakeholder groups feel involved. In this context we are thinking of the staff, pupils, parents, governors, external support staff and, of course, the community at large. There is strong evidence that the most successful schools are those that encourage all these groups to become involved. Patterns of working and organizational procedures are important factors here, as are the attitudes of those involved. The activities on the following pages can be used to review existing procedures for involving these groups in school activities.

Briefing

Aims

- To encourage a review of the extent to which existing procedures encourage the involvement of pupils, parents and staff.

- To consider how these procedures might be improved.

Process

We provide three activities here, separately addressing procedures relating to pupils, parents and staff. Together the three activities could be used as the basis of a staff development day around the theme of involvement. Alternatively the activities could be used individually on separate occasions.

It is also possible to use the three activities as the basis of a 'jigsaw' activity. This involves separate groups looking at one activity. Later new groups are formed involving individuals who have taken part in the three different activities. Within those second groups members describe the findings and outcomes of their earlier discussions and then consider the likely implication. This jigsaw approach is a particularly effective way of involving staff in detailed discussions of a range of topics in a relatively short amount of time.

Add some arguments of your own to the following table:

PUPIL INVOLVEMENT SHOULD		
ENHANCE PUPILS' LEARNING OUTCOMES		GIVE PUPILS MORE CHOICE
ENSURE THAT LEARNING OBJECTIVES ARE UNDERSTOOD		PROVIDE FEEDBACK ON THE EFFECTIVENESS OF TEACHING
	RAISE SELF-ESTEEM	INVOLVE PUPILS IN RECORD-KEEPING

Step 2

Compare your table with a colleague. See if you can agree the *three* most important arguments.

Step 3

Compare your choices with other pairs.

Step 4

In the light of this discussion about pupil involvement I intend to . . .

....

....

....

....

....

....

....

....

....

....

....

....

....

....

....

....

....

....

Encouraging participation of parents

In small groups review the school's procedures in the light of 'The Wheel'.

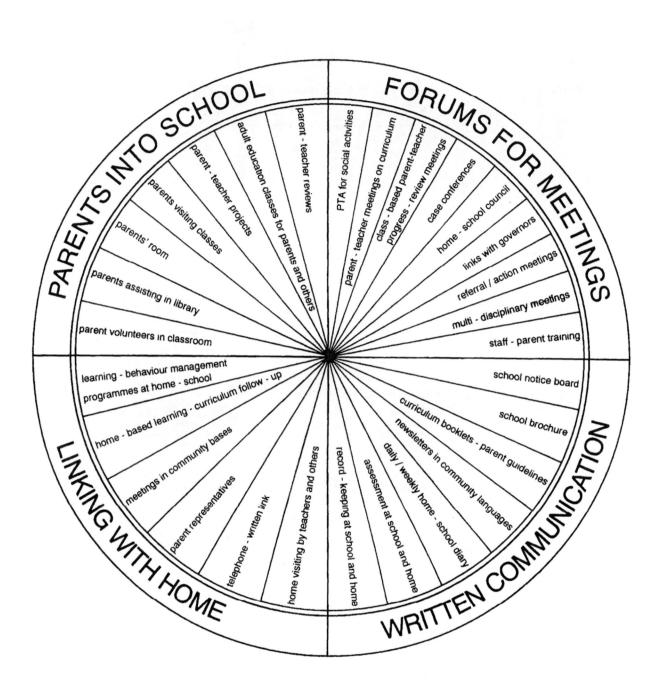

The wheel contains four quadrants:

PARENTS INTO SCHOOL
- parent - teacher reviews
- adult education classes for parents and others
- parent - teacher projects
- parents visiting classes
- parents' room
- parents assisting in library
- parent volunteers in classroom

FORUMS FOR MEETINGS
- PTA for social activities
- parent - teacher meetings on curriculum
- class - based parent-teacher progress - review meetings
- case conferences
- home - school council
- links with governors
- referral / action meetings
- multi - disciplinary meetings
- staff - parent training

LINKING WITH HOME
- learning - behaviour management programmes at home - school
- home - based learning - curriculum follow - up
- meetings in community bases
- parent representatives
- telephone - written link
- home visiting by teachers and others

WRITTEN COMMUNICATION
- school notice board
- school brochure
- curriculum booklets - parent guidelines
- newsletters in community languages
- daily / weekly home - school diary
- assessment at school and home
- record - keeping at school and home

Source: Adapted from Wolfendale, S., 1987.

Reviewing parental involvement in schools

1. Do you know the school policy for contacting/meeting parents?

2. Are the parent involvement procedures arrived at by joint consensus?

3. Is there a record-keeping system of parent contacts?

4. Is there a method for evaluating parent contacts?

5. Is time made available for staff to discuss with parents?

6. Is information routinely provided for parents?

7. Do parents have opportunities to meet and discuss together?

8. Is there a physical parent base in the school?

9. Is there a clear written statement of parent involvement available to staff and parents?

10. Are parents seen as individuals and given individual attention?

11. Do interactions between staff and parents indicate mutual respect and equality as opposed to professional distancing created by the idea of the 'expert'?

12. Is information provided to parents which helps them evaluate:
    i) school attainments generally?
    ii) own child attainments?

13. Does the school project a welcoming, valuing image for child and parent?

14. Is there flexibility in ways to involve parents?

15. Is parent involvement largely problem-orientated?

16. Are school records on families open to parent inspection?

Encouraging involvement of staff

Think about recent changes in your school. How do you feel about these developments? Consider the two lists of statements below and tick *one* in *each* list that is nearest to your own view.

RESPONSES TO CHANGE: LIST 1 – COMMITMENT

At the present time all schools are making many changes to different aspects of school life. What has been your reaction to recent changes which have been initiated by your school?

Here are five views expressed by teachers on their response to school-initiated changes. Which is the closest to yours? Tick the one that gives the best match.

A I have very mixed feelings about most of the recent changes. Some I like and I think will help to improve things. To me others just seem daft or irrelevant and so frankly are a waste of time and energy. Right now, I'm not sure what I think about the changes as a whole. ☐

B I object very strongly to most of the changes. It's not just that they haven't been thought through: most of them are actually misguided and make things worse. In my view we shouldn't be afraid to oppose the changes whenever and wherever we can. ☐

C I don't agree fully with all the changes. But things often turn out better than they seem at first. In such circumstances the thing to do is make the best of it. There'll probably be some real benefits later on, and I prefer to be optimistic about that. ☐

D I don't think most of them have been adequately tried out. This is not a very professional way to make changes. But with many we've been given no choice so, for the most part, I don't feel any real commitment. ☐

E Most of the changes we're making will prove to be very worthwhile in the end. Some won't work and will have to be dropped or revised – that's inevitable when you do something new. But I'm confident the benefits will outweigh the drawbacks. ☐

© 1994 Cambridge University

RESPONSES TO CHANGE: LIST 2 – CONTROL

Here are another five views expressed by teachers on their reaction to recent school-initiated changes. Once again, which is the closest to yours? Tick the one that gives the best match.

F Wherever the changes come from you can always bend quite a lot of them to your own purposes if you set your mind to it. The room for manoeuvre may be limited, but it gives you some control to do it your way, I think.

G It's a mixed bag, in my view. Many changes are being imposed, and some we like, some we don't. Then there are changes we've chosen for ourselves. Some of the imposed ones might be altered in the light of experience, I suppose.

H I feel virtually all the changes are being imposed from above and we're left to implement them in a rather mechanistic way. There's far too little room for us to adapt them to our own circumstances and I don't like the thought of having to learn to live with them.

I Whatever we do here in terms of change has to be related to our own ideas of where the school's going. Some changes fit better than others, but in the end the real control lies with us, not with those who dream up the ideas.

J The trend is for most changes to be top-down and that makes me feel I don't have much control. So, in the end, all you can do is concentrate on the few you approve of, and put up with the rest.

© 1994 Cambridge University

Step 8   You can plot your score on this table:

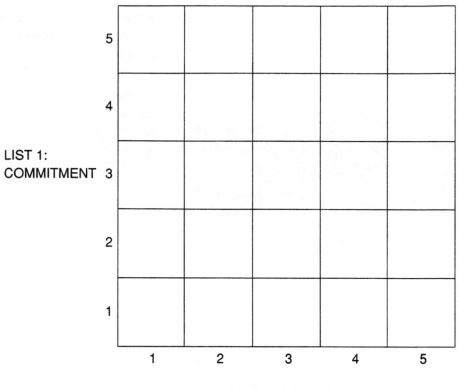

LIST 2: CONTROL

SCORING KEY

LIST 1	LIST 2
F = 4	A = 3
G = 3	B = 1
H = 1	C = 4
I = 5	D = 2
J = 2	E = 5

Step 9   Compare your results with some colleagues. You may even like to put everybody's scores on one master sheet. What do the scores tell you? Do staff feel involved in what is going on? Do they have some control? Are they committed? Consider what actions, if any, are necessary, and by whom.

© IQEA – Creating the Conditions for School Improvement

Activity 5.3: Creating a Climate of Access

Context

While policies and procedures that encourage involvement are necessary, ultimately much depends upon the relationships that develop within and around the school community. What matters is how people relate to one another as they interact when carrying out their day-to-day tasks. Following are some incidents of the sort that occur regularly in school. Choose some of the incidents and discuss how you would respond with a few of your colleagues.

Briefing

Aims

- To encourage staff to consider a variety of day-to-day events that are indicative of a school's climate.

- To consider possible ways of increasing the openness of the school.

Process

Page 54 should be copied to make 12 separate 'cards'. Choose the ones that seem most relevant to the school.

For Step 1 small groups of staff are formed. Each group is asked to consider one situation. They are required to agree what action should be taken in the light of what has occurred. Each group presents its situation and describes the recommended response to the other groups of staff. Having heard this presentation, attention is focused on how this compares with existing school practice. The process can be repeated.

Following these discussions, Step 2 involves individuals reflecting upon their own position and writing some notes. Finally during Step 3 small groups compare their ideas and go on to propose some actions that should be taken.

1. A parent governor asks about the policy for pupil induction

2. A supervisor is angry because a pupil does not return her tray to the hatch after lunch

3. A mother regularly watches the playground because she is worried that her son is being bullied

4. A group of governors asks for criteria for judging effective teaching

5. Some teachers never speak in staff meetings

6. A group of pupils tells the local newspaper that nobody listens to their complaints

7. A parent complains that his son's book has not been marked

8. Staff say that they are not told what is discussed at senior management meetings

9. The classroom assistants have requested a separate staff room

10. Pupils ask for a student council to be formed

11. A parent ignores the sign stating that she should wait for her child at the gate

12. The educational psychologist says that staff have no time to talk about individual children with her

Step 2   Complete the following statement:

> *We could make the climate of this school*
> *more open by...*

....

....

....

....

....

....

....

....

....

....

....

....

....

....

Step 3

Compare your views with your colleagues. Agree some actions that should be taken.

Context

Our experience shows that the involvement of support agencies *can* strengthen the work of a school. This exercise will help you to consider how much you are already drawing upon outside help. It will also help you to identify areas where it may be helpful to draw on further support. You will also need to think about how 'outsiders' can make an effective impact on teaching and learning.

Briefing

Aims

- To review the involvement of support agencies.

- To work in usual school teams to develop strategies for making more effective use of support agencies.

Process

Following an introduction to the topic, Step 1 involves each participant in completing the form regarding the involvement of outside agencies. It may be, of course, that some colleagues have little or nothing to record at this stage. Step 2 involves participants in comparing their completed forms. These discussions should help participants to recognize the types of involvement that occur.

During Step 3, groups address three questions that are intended to encourage a more evaluative discussion. The questions focus first on the general level of impact upon the school and then, more specifically, on their impact upon classroom practice. Finally the groups consider what factors facilitate the effective use of external agencies.

For Step 4, staff are asked to meet with members of their usual working groups (e.g., year teams, department) to plan a strategy for involving support agencies. These discussions should be as specific as possible, e.g. who should we target? What can we do in the next few weeks to make their work more effective?

Step 1   Working on your own make a list of outside agencies that you have had contact with in the past. Make a note also of the purposes of this contact.

OUTSIDE AGENCY	PURPOSES OF CONTACT

Step 2   Either in pairs or small groups compare your lists with colleagues.

Step 3   In your groups consider the following questions, making your own notes about the outcomes of these discussions.

- What contributions do support agencies make to the school?

- Do they ever have an impact on teaching and learning?

- What arrangements help outside agencies to make an effective contribution to the improvement of teaching and learning?

Step 4   Move into your usual working groups (e.g., year teams, departments). Target one support agency and plan a strategy for involving them during the next few weeks.

© IQEA – Creating the Conditions for School Improvement

CHAPTER 6

Staff Development

Schools will not improve unless teachers, individually and collectively, develop. Teacher growth is at the heart of school development. While teachers can often develop their practice on an individual basis, if the whole school is to develop then there need to be many opportunities for the staff to learn together. Collaborative learning need not be something extra to do; it can often occur as part of teachers working together. However, it is crucial that staff development activities are, in the main, focused on the classroom. Staff development programmes need to help teachers develop as teachers and as analysts of the pupils' learning.

6.1 Professional learning is central to school improvement.
6.2 The school needs a policy for staff development.
6.3 Staff development should be classroom focused.
6.4 The school should be organized for professional learning.

Staff Development: Overview

We take a broad view of staff development. It is collaborative as well as personal. It takes place away from the school site but more often at school. It occurs during special and formal development events but also informally as part and parcel of your work. Given that a great deal of staff development is school-based, we believe that there are four aspects worth paying attention to.

First, we need to recognize that staff development is essential to school improvement. In other words, your school will not grow unless the staff develop. So saying, it is not enough to hope colleagues will develop. We say this because colleagues need planned opportunities to learn. Moreover, teachers' professional learning needs to be related to and reflect the school's priorities for development. Staff development should be both systematic and linked to the school's development plan.

Second, it follows from the first that your school should have a policy for staff development. This policy should:

- focus on the school's needs;
- use teacher appraisal to provide links between individual needs and the whole school;

- establish every teacher's right to professional development;
- create and sustain a framework for staff to disseminate their new knowledge and skills;
- coordinate information on external courses;
- review the design of staff training days and evaluate their relevance and effectiveness;
- ensure staff development is included in the school's budget and timetable.

Unless there is an active policy for professional learning which is carefully managed and monitored, then teachers' development will not be integrated with school improvement.

Third, although staff development may attend to a large number of topics and needs, fundamentally a development programme should aim to enhance the quality of pupil learning. For this reason, staff development needs to be classroom focused. Teachers need to develop by looking at their teaching and by observing the learners. While teachers often have many development needs – especially when they take on extra responsibilities – they nevertheless need to keep on developing their classroom skills and understandings. Indeed, unless staff development yields improvements in teaching and learning, then the school will not improve as a school.

Fourth, it follows from these three points that the school should be regarded as a context for professional learning. The school's organization will influence how staff interact, who they collaborate with and how much time they have to work together. The school's organizational structure powerfully influences whether staff can learn with and from one another. Furthermore, the organizational culture of the school has a direct and indirect bearing on how much staff share ideas, successes and setbacks.

If the school is to be a community of learners then attention needs to be devoted to these four aspects of staff development.

Activity 6.1: Professional Learning

Context

Staff development is vital to the growth of the school. Unless staff develop the school will not improve. While this statement can be simply expressed we know that in practice the processes of staff development are complex, subtle and can take many forms. Moreover, teachers need to agree a set of principles for their professional learning if they are to make the school into a community of learners.

Briefing

Aims

- To facilitate the sharing and agreeing of a common set of ideas about professional learning in your school.

Process

First give out copies of the 'Nine Statements about Professional Learning' to all participants, having photocopied Appendix p. 132 and made up sets of cards for each participant. Tell participants they need to arrange them into a diamond pattern at each step. Then invite colleagues to embark on Step 1.

Step 2 involves sharing with a partner. Emphasize that it is the *reasons* which matter as well as the position of the statement cards.

Step 3 involves the pairs working with another pair. Encourage participants to come to an agreed diamond on the basis of reasons – not by negotiating deals or trading. Step 3 is repeated in Steps 4 and 5.

At the end of the activity see if you are now close to, or clearer about, what your school's staff development policy should encompass.

You should individually read and reflect on the nine statements set out below and on the nine cards distributed to you by the course leader. (These statements appear on Appendix p. 132.) Now arrange the cards into a diamond pattern like this:

```
            1
        2       2
    3       3       3
        4       4
            5
```

The statements should be in priority order where 1 is of highest priority and the statement at 5 is, for you, the lowest priority statement.

NINE STATEMENTS ABOUT PROFESSIONAL LEARNING

- The most important learning opportunities available to teachers are in the school.

- INSET courses play a major role in school improvement.

- You really need an expert to tell you what to do.

- Teachers should always continue to learn about teaching and classroom processes.

- Professional learning should be determined by individual teachers working on their own.

- The staff's professional development needs to be carefully managed and coordinated.

- Staff development days are valuable opportunities for professional learning.

- Teacher appraisal offers many opportunities for professional learning.

- Professional learning is a collaborative activity.

Step 2

Now share your diamond with a partner.
Look at one another's.

Explain to each other your *reasons* for putting the statements in your respective patterns.
Having articulated your reasons, next combine your ideas and put together an agreed single diamond.

Step 3

You and your partner should find another pair and repeat Step 2.

This time, you can substitute ONE statement of your own (as a four) for one of the original given propositions.

Step 4

As a group of four now share your diamond with another foursome's.

Again:
Look at the two diamonds; compare and contrast.
One group explain your reasons, then the other.
Now, try to compile a single diamond.

This time, you can substitute THREE statements of your own (as a group) for any of the propositions in your two diamonds.

Step 5

Now review the diamonds that have been created by the groups.

Is it possible to produce an overall set of statements about professional learning in the school?

What do the higher priority statements reveal about the ways the staff approach and understand professional learning?

From these statements, is it possible to develop a staff development policy?

Activity 6.2: Learning Needs Analysis

Context

In Chapter 4 we emphasized the need for plans and planning. Here we want to elaborate on the idea of planning by suggesting that any plans for improvement should be linked to staff development needs and priorities. Attention must be paid to staff development since it is through the staff's growth that changes occur and the school advances.

Briefing

Aim

- To consider the staff development implications and actions of an agreed change in your school.

Process

There are five steps to this activity. Step 1 is a relatively straightforward decision. If there is more than one suggestion different groups could work on different priorities. Equally, you might want to first take a development which is a high priority in the school's development plan. Step 2 should take some time. Invite colleagues to be as specific as possible since this will be of help in Steps 3, 4 and 5.

Step 3 is a critical phase in the activity. The list we offer is not exhaustive and you should add to it. Step 4 builds on Step 3, and Step 5 asks participants to create from their previous thinking a suggested programme of activities.

This activity is probably best attempted over a morning or whole INSET day.

Step 1

> Identify a specific change you are currently working on as a whole staff, department or key stage team. What do you want to see happening when the change has been implemented?

Step 2

> In order to make the change happen what do *staff* (i.e., teachers and others) need to do differently? Itemize these actions below:

Step 3

> To assist staff, what kinds of support and development opportunities do they need? You might want to use the categories below or use some of your own devising.
>
> Information
>
> Opportunities to share with others their thoughts about the change
>
> Opportunities to show and reflect on their experience of trying to make the change happen
>
> Workshops to develop skills
>
> Support from a colleague
>
> Opportunities to see the change working successfully
>
> Resources
>
> INSET courses to promote understanding
>
> INSET courses to provide skills
>
> External consultancy brought in
>
> Time to reflect and take stock

Step 4

Using the same lists as in Step 3, now move from looking at the kinds of support staff needed, to focusing on which individuals/ groups need which kinds of support.

You might do this as a two-part activity:

Part 1: On your own make a list showing who will need what kinds of support.

Part 2: Compare your list with those of your colleagues.

Step 5

In the light of these discussions, evaluate the school's current arrangements for supporting staff in respect of the change identified in Step 1.

© IQEA – Creating the Conditions for School Improvement

Activity 6.3: Taking Staff Development into Classrooms

Context

Staff development activities, however stimulating, are unlikely to have an impact unless teachers are provided with support as they explore new approaches in the context of their own classrooms. Too often staff development occurs away from the usual context in which teaching takes place and, indeed, is led by people who have not visited the specific contexts in which their participants have to operate. One writer noted that this is akin to a basketball coach giving advice to a team he has never seen play.

Probably the most powerful form of classroom support is where pairs of colleagues enter into a partnership with the intention of exploring developments in practice. However, such partnerships have to be set up with considerable care.

Briefing

Aims

- To examine the use of classroom partnerships.

- To begin to work towards establishing some partnerships in your school.

Process

The activity consists of four steps. Step 1 is a 'tuning in' session; it raises awareness. If colleagues have had previous experience of such partnerships encourage them to share their insights.

Step 2 is a more active session. It aims to stimulate discussion and problem solving. Step 3 is a sharing activity. Encourage colleagues to fully share their ideas and to search for similarities and differences amongst their proposals.

Step 4 is not only a summarizing stage; colleagues should also try to devise some action points for developing partnerships in their school.

Copies of pages 68 and 69 (The Partnership Framework) should be distributed and read prior to the sessions. These are used to underpin group discussions of the important features of classroom partnerships.

Step 1:
The
Partnership
Framework

(i) Purpose of the partnership

The first step is to think about what you hope to achieve through working in partnership. Your choice of a partner may depend upon this. Some partnerships may, as part of a particular school initiative, have a tightly focused aim (e.g., to evaluate the implementation of some new curriculum materials). Others may prefer a more open-ended approach, valuing the opportunity to learn from others through working together, without a specific focus in mind. Both kinds of partnerships can stimulate worthwhile developments. What is important is that these purposes should have been discussed, and that both partners are clear about one another's intentions.

(ii) Ways of using a partner

There are a number of ways of using a partner to help you develop your work. In the early stages, a partner may be used to help you to identify aspects of your teaching which you wish to review. Once a partnership is established, a partner may be used to provide support in exploring new approaches. A partner's function may include:

- acting as a 'mirror', reflecting back to you what they see happening in your classroom;
- observing and recording more specific events or processes, such as individual participation in group work;
- helping to make sense of observations and generate new questions about aspects of teaching;
- helping to formulate new ideas for further development.

(iii) Choosing a partner

Your choice of partner will be influenced by the purpose of the partnership. It is important to choose somebody with whom you can work comfortably. It could be:

- a member of your own department
- a member of another curriculum area
- a member of another year team
- a member of another school
- a member of the support team
- other members of the school.

Your choice of partner will also be influenced by timetabling considerations, cover available and other practical constraints. Pupils may also be involved as partners. Their perceptions can provide important insights into their own learning and what is happening in the classroom.

(iv) Involving a third person

Sometimes partnerships decide to involve a third person:

- as a sounding board for ideas
- to help overcome 'sticking points'
- to give encouragement
- to provide strategies to promote decision making
- to minute discussion if requested
- to participate in observation
- to help focus on learning within the class
- to challenge perceptions.

The third person could be

- a member of the senior management team
- a departmental member
- a member of the support services
- another member of the school.

(v) Establishing ground rules

Partnerships need to establish guidelines and agree upon partners' responsibilities towards one another and towards others who may have an interest or involvement in the work. Partners have a responsibility to:

- work together in a spirit of cooperation, equality, openness, trust, reliability, respect and mutual support;
- fulfil their commitments towards one another within the partnership as initially discussed and agreed;
- maintain confidentiality relating to all aspects of the partnership work;
- inform (and where appropriate seek permission of) students, parents, colleagues and governors about the nature and purposes of the work.

Step 2

Form into groups of four or five. Each group is asked to consider one of the situations below and then to:

- Formulate a plan as to how a partnership framework might be used in this situation.
- Also ask each member of the group to keep their own notes of the plan they devise as a group.

SITUATIONS

1. Two teachers have agreed to help one another with difficulties they are experiencing with particular pupils in their classes. In both instances the pupils concerned are disruptive to the usual pattern of classroom activities.

2. Following a series of staff development sessions a teacher has asked a colleague to assist in the introduction of group work in the classroom. Specifically the teacher is uncertain of what her role should be during group activities.

3. As a result of a recent school inspection a group of teachers have been asked to review the use of talk in their classrooms. The inspectors had reported that this was an area of general weakness.

4. Having heard about the value of partnerships as a means of staff development, two teachers decide that they want to give it a try. At this stage neither of them has specific issues that they wish to address.

Step 3

> When every group has completed Step 2, reform the groups in such a way that each member of the new group has a plan for a different situation.
>
> Each member now describes their situation, presents their plans and invites questions and discussion.

Step 4

> Each group should now agree a summary of the key lessons that have emerged.
>
> Then they should discuss how they might develop their own partnership in this school.

Activity 6.4: Schools as Learning Organizations

Context

Successful schools are organized in order to create the conditions in which all members of the organization come to see themselves as learners. An assumption is that fostering the professional learning of adults has a payoff in terms of the ways in which they come to foster the learning of their pupils and one another. Schools need to be communities of learners where adults and pupils are learning and developing.

Briefing

Aim

• To encourage participants to examine the extent to which your school's organizational structures and processes facilitate staff development.

Process

Step 1 is an individual activity. Participants might be given 20–30 minutes to fill in their responses in private.

Step 2 involves two closely linked tasks. The first is to share their responses to Step 1. Second, in the light of these responses the group should try to formulate some proposals for developing the school as a learning organization. The latter should be recorded for Step 3.

Step 4 seeks to move from ideas to action. You will need to determine in advance what will happen to the groups' suggestions.

Make some notes about the following:

1. Are there effective strategies for supporting staff in addressing the problems they face in their work?

2. Are all staff involved in activities to foster their thinking and practice?

3. Do in-service activities support teachers in developing classroom practice?

4. Are staff development activities linked to school development practices?

5. Do staff collaborate in supporting one another's learning?

6. Is effective use made of consultants to support staff development?

Step 2

Work in groups to compare your responses to these questions. Formulate some proposals for developing the school as a 'learning organization'.

Step 3

All the groups come together for a plenary reporting back session to construct a set of agreed proposals for developing the school as a learning organization.

Step 4

Move back into the same groups as before. Allow 10 minutes for groups to write down answers to these questions:

Q.1 What should now be done?

Q.2 By whom?

Q.3 By when?

Response sheets should be handed to the organizer of the activity.

© IQEA – Creating the Conditions for School Improvement

CHAPTER 7

Coordination

During a typical day in school so many things happen. As a result staff sometimes complain about not knowing what is happening until the last minute. The coordination of activities is an important way of keeping people involved, particularly when changes of policy are being introduced. Communication within the school is an important aspect of coordination, as are the informal interactions that occur.

The activities in this chapter will help you and your colleagues to consider the following ideas:

7.1 Coordinators have to develop skills in working with colleagues.
7.2 Staff working groups can be effective mechanisms for coordinating development initiatives.
7.3 Systems of communication need to be carefully planned and monitored.
7.4 Dialogue about teaching is essential to the improvement of practice.

Coordination: Overview

Schools are not just buildings, curricula and procedures such as timetables. *Much more importantly* schools comprise relationships and interactions among often quite large groups of people. How these interpersonal interactions are carried out largely determines how successful a school is in achieving its purposes.

In the literature on educational management schools are sometimes referred to as 'loosely coupled systems'. This loose coupling occurs because schools consist of units, processes, actions and individuals that tend to operate in isolation from one another. Loose coupling is also encouraged by the goal ambiguity that characterizes schooling. Despite the rhetoric of curriculum aims and objectives, schools consist of groups of people who may have very different values and, indeed, beliefs about the purposes of schooling. One writer has used the metaphor of football to illustrate the point. He describes a school as a soccer game in which players enter and leave the pitch at will, and attempt to kick the ball towards several goals that are scattered haphazardly around an oval, sloping field.

How, then, can such an organization be coordinated in order that those involved can work in a more efficient way? It does seem that relationships are the key to establishing greater coordination.

School relationships can be structured in one of three ways: individualistically, competitively or cooperatively. In schools with an individualistic form of organization teachers tend to work alone to achieve goals unrelated to the goals of their colleagues. Consequently there is little sense of common purpose, no sharing of expertise and limited support for individuals. Furthermore such schools often move towards a more competitive form of organization.

In a competitive system teachers strive to do better than their colleagues, recognizing that their fates are negatively linked. Here the career of one teacher is likely to be enhanced by the failure of others within the school. In this win–lose struggle to succeed it is almost inevitable that individuals will celebrate difficulties experienced by their colleagues since they are likely to increase their own chances of success.

Clearly, therefore, the organizational approach which is most likely to create a positive working atmosphere within a school is one that emphasizes cooperation. In such a school individuals are more likely to strive for mutual benefit, recognizing that they all share a common purpose and, indeed, a common fate. Furthermore, individuals know that their performance can be influenced positively by the performance of others. This being the case, individuals feel proud when a colleague succeeds and is recognized for professional competence.

A school that is based upon a cooperative structure is likely to make good use of the expertise of all its personnel, provide sources of stimulation and enrichment that will foster their professional development, and encourage positive attitudes to the introduction of new ways of working. In short, it is well on the way to becoming a learning-enriched school.

Having said all of that, a word of warning is necessary. Establishing a cooperative way of working is not a simple matter, not least because it is necessary to do so in ways that do not reduce the discretion of individual teachers. Teaching is a complex and often unpredictable business that requires a degree of improvisation. Teachers must have sufficient autonomy to make instant decisions that take account of the individuality of their pupils and the uniqueness of every encounter that occurs. What is needed, therefore, is a well coordinated, cooperative style of working that gives individual teachers the confidence to improvise in a search for the most appropriate responses to the situations they meet. In other words, we are seeking to create a more tightly coupled system without losing loose coupling benefits.

In this chapter we look at the following ways in which schools can encourage greater coordination:

- the establishment of skilful coordinators
- using task groups to get things done
- the establishment of communication networks
- facilitating discussion of practice.

Activity 7.1: Being a Coordinator

Context

In recent years the need for schools to deal with multiple innovations has meant that many staff now have to take on the role of coordinator. Unfortunately, little attention has been paid to helping individuals to develop the necessary skills for carrying out this part of their work.

A coordinator needs to have clear views, but also be able to listen to, and accommodate, the views of others. This flexibility will enable the coordinator to judge when to move things on, when to be willing to change the agenda and when to provide time and space for staff to explore ways forward. This implies that the coordinator will have a strong sense of personal security. Their function ought not to be that of control, but rather to be a guide to staff as they seek to participate in constructive developmental activity. This guidance will be based upon:

- the coordinator's perspective of the overall aims and plans which exist in the school;
- the coordinator's knowledge of areas of developmental activity and expertise already in existence in the school;
- the coordinator's awareness of, and contact with, individuals and agencies which can provide external support and expertise.

A sensitive use of influence can often move people in directions which they would not themselves have chosen, but in directions which can be of greater benefit both to the school and to the individuals concerned. Above all, the coordinator needs to be involved in the activities of the group in order that empathy exists, so that he or she can show encouragement, and generate self-confidence within each member of the group.

Briefing

Aims

- To encourage staff to consider key skill areas involved in acting as a coordinator.
- To help individuals to prepare an action plan for developing their skills.

Process

Participants should read the introductory text and discuss the types of coordination tasks they carry out. This helps to focus the more specific discussion about skills involved in such work that follows.

During Step 1 participants consider the list of eight skills. They are asked to write some notes about their own work with respect to these items. This is followed by intensive discussion between pairs of colleagues. After a period of such discussion the partners assist one another in preparing an action plan. At this stage it may be appropriate for partners to consider extending their work together, as a means of providing coaching once the action plan is implemented. Suggestions for how partnerships can be created for this purpose are provided in Chapter 5.

Step 1

Research suggests that the following skills seem to be important to success in coordinating groups of adults in the development of practice. Make some notes about your own skills in these areas.

SKILLS OF THE COORDINATOR

1. Developing a clear purpose for activities

2. Establishing rapport with colleagues

3. Leading meetings and other group activities

4. Maintaining interest and enthusiasm

© IQEA – Creating the Conditions for School Improvement

5. Solving problems, including difficulties over relationships

6. Encouraging collaboration

7. Providing support

8. Keeping people informed

Step 2

Having completed your notes form a partnership with a colleague. Plan how you would assist one another in developing your skills as coordinators.

Step 3

Action Plan

Make some notes of actions that you plan to take to develop your skills as a coordinator.

1. My goals are...

2. To achieve these goals I intend to...

3. The problems I anticipate are...

4. I will seek support from...

© IQEA – Creating the Conditions for School Improvement

Activity 7.2: Task Groups

Context

Some decisions that schools face can be made by the governors or management team on their own. Other decisions may be made in a staff meeting after a few minutes of discussion. There are decisions, however, that require much longer consideration before a recommendation can be formulated. In particular, school-wide issues call for careful review and planning involving the whole staff.

One strategy is to appoint a task group representing the whole school that is given the responsibility for considering the problem and planning the actions that the staff need to take. For such a group to be successful it needs to be given clear goals, a schedule, and the resources necessary for it to function. Membership of such a group may be on a voluntary basis, but sometimes teachers are asked and expected to serve.

Teachers are empowered to solve school-wide problems when they are placed into task groups. Their task is to review, plan, recommend and support the implementation of solutions to school-wide issues and problems. In effect they become a small problem-solving group that:

* defines a problem or issue;
* gathers data about the nature, causes and extent of the problem or issue;
* considers a variety of alternative actions and solutions;
* makes conclusions and summarizes them into a recommendation;
* presents and advocates the recommendations to the staff as a whole;
* oversees implementation after the staff as a whole decides whether to accept or modify the task group's recommendations.

Briefing

Aims

* To consider some principles for using task groups effectively and to get staff to evaluate current practices.
* To generate some guidelines that can be used to make future task groups more effective.

Process

Before carrying out the activities staff are asked to read the 'Task Groups' description, above. They are then introduced to the five points in Step 1 regarding school-wide task groups and how they can be made effective.

Step 2 is carried out in small groups. Members of these groups are asked to recall a task group of which they were members. Using the form provided they reflect upon the work of this group. Then each group member tells their story to the others.

Following these discussions, Step 3 requires each group to generate guidelines as to how future task groups in the school can be made more effective. Finally these recommendations are reported to other groups.

Step 1

Discuss the following propositions:

To be effective a school-wide task group requires

1. Valid and complete information about the problem or issue.
2. Enough intellectual conflict and disagreement to ensure that all potential solutions get a fair hearing.
3. A method of analysis and synthesis that generates ideas for solutions.
4. Free and informed choice.
5. Continuing motivation to solve the problem if the implemented plan does not work.

Step 2

Consider your experience of a task group in school. Evaluate the effectiveness of its work using the form below.

	YES	NO
There was valid and complete information available		
Disagreements allowed different points of view to be heard		
Discussions generated positive ways forward		
Individuals were able to influence outcomes		
Group members maintained their involvement even when problems arose		

In the light of this analysis, work with colleagues to generate some guidelines for making task groups effective. Share these recommendations with the other groups.

Activity 7.3: Communication Networks

Context

The issue of communication is a vital component of overall school coordination, particularly when there are changes to be made. In order to organize itself to accomplish its goals, maintain itself in good working order and, at the same time, adapt to changing circumstances, sound procedures for communication are essential to the school. Meetings must be scheduled; reports from task groups distributed; departmental meetings organized; summaries of various activities need to be written and sent round to all staff. All of these responses are structured communication opportunities. The communication network thus created determines the amount and type of information a member of staff will receive from colleagues.

Schools working on improvement activities must, therefore, seek to create an effective communication network. In particular this should be geared to making all staff aware of progress related to project activities and decisions that require them to take particular actions.

Effective communication within a school is essential during improvement initiatives. No amount of good thinking by itself will address the ubiquitous problem of faulty communication. Since change is a highly personal experience, and since schools consist of numerous individuals and groups undergoing different (to them) experiences, no single communication is going to reassure or clarify the meaning of change for everyone. It does seem that people will misinterpret and misunderstand some aspect of the purpose or practice of something that is new to them.

To be successful in coordinating developments in school, therefore, it is necessary to work at communication. A study of the theory of change indicates the importance of frequent, personal interactions as a key to success. Indeed, two-way communication about specific innovations that are being attempted is a requirement of success. To the extent that the information flow is accurate, the problems get identified. This means that each person's perceptions and concerns get aired.

Briefing

Aims

- To encourage staff to recognize the importance of communication within a school and to seek out their roles in establishing effective mechanisms.

- To use the technique of 'brainstorming' to generate some ideas for improving communication systems within the school.

Process

The focus of the discussion is established by asking participants to read the 'Communication networks' description, above.

Participants are then told that the aim is to generate some positive proposals for improving communication in the school. They are asked to include in their considerations the question of their own role within such developments.

At this stage it is helpful to write the key question on a blackboard or flip-chart sheet (i.e., 'How can we improve communication in our school?').

Groups of approximately five persons are created. Each group has a large piece of paper and felt tip pen. One member is asked to be the scribe. The rules of 'brainstorming' are explained. This is a cost-effective way of getting a list of good ideas based on all the experience within a working group.

Brainstorming goes on for no more than five minutes. The list of ideas produced now represents an agenda for general discussion within the group. Finally each group reports its conclusions to the other groups.

Reviewing the School's Communication System

Form small working groups and 'brainstorm' proposals for improving existing arrangements in school.

RULES FOR BRAINSTORMING

Brainstorming is valuable in creating an agenda for discussion. It involves a set period when participants suggest points or comments relating to the area under discussion. One member of the group records these contributions, preferably on a blackboard or flip chart. Strict rules are kept during the brainstorming in order that participants feel confident to make their suggestions without fear of criticism. Essential rules are as follows:

- all ideas related to the issue in any direct way are desired
- the maximum number of related ideas is desired
- one idea may be modified, adapted and expressed as another idea
- ideas should be expressed as clearly and concisely as possible
- no discussion of the ideas should be attempted
- no criticism of ideas is accepted.

Once the brainstorming is over, the list of points generated provides an agenda for normal discussion. Share your conclusions with other working groups.

© IQEA – Creating the Conditions for School Improvement

Context

There is a great deal of evidence that a feature of successful schools is an emphasis on teachers talking about their practice. To encourage this dialogue, quality time is set aside that provides opportunities for such discussion to take place.

Briefing

Aims

- To provide an opportunity for staff to review the extent to which they have opportunities to talk about their practice with colleagues.

- To develop some strategies for encouraging more of this type of discussion.

Process

Initially attention is drawn to the importance of talk as a means of helping teachers to reflect upon and develop their practice in the light of experience. In Step 1 staff are asked to work with appropriate colleagues (e.g., existing partnerships, year teams or department groups), using the form provided to review the role of talk in their day-to-day work. The form is in three stages. At each stage individuals record their responses to the question before having discussion with colleagues.

Once all those questions have been addressed the groups move on to Step 2 which invites them to review how more discussion about teaching could be arranged. Finally, in Step 3, each person writes a memo to themselves about actions that need to be taken.

Step 1   Working in pairs, year teams or department groups use the following questions to review the forms of talking that go on. For each question allow each person to write their notes in private *before* discussion takes place.

REVIEWING TALK

1. When do you talk to colleagues?

When you have made your list put a code against each item as follows:
S = social talk; P = professional talk.

2. Which of the items marked 'P' address directly issues about your teaching?

3. How much of the talking about teaching occurs as a result of formal interactions (e.g., department meetings)? How much occurs during informal discussions?

© *IQEA – Creating the Conditions for School Improvement*

Step 2

Having carried out this review discuss how opportunities for discussion of teaching might be improved.

Step 3

On your own complete the following memo in the light of this activity.

Memo
To help me in developing my teaching I need...

....

....

....

....

....

....

....

....

....

....

....

....

....

....

....

....

....

....

CHAPTER 8

Leadership

In our work with schools we have consistently identified the way leadership is conceptualized and perceived within the school as a factor influencing its capacity to cope with change and undertake improvement work. Those schools addressing leadership as a major area for reform, and moving from transactional to transformational models, are maximizing capacity by:

8.1 Establishing a clear vision for the school.
8.2 Valuing and utilizing task-relevant experience.
8.3 Building consensus without sacrificing critical thinking.
8.4 Accepting that leadership is a function to which many staff contribute, rather than a set of responsibilities vested in a single individual.

Leadership: Overview

Recent changes in legislation have significantly altered the management role at school level. As a consequence, the majority of schools now pay more (and more explicit) attention to management structures, processes and roles. There is a danger that this focus on management as a technical process, though in itself an important and much needed development, can be associated with an over-reliance on 'systems' and a corresponding decrease in the amount of attention given to those aspects of the school which unite and inspire human effort. Such aspects can be grouped together under the term leadership – which refers to the processes used to influence groups of staff towards achieving common goals.

There is considerable evidence in the studies of school effectiveness that leadership is a key element in determining school success. Perhaps such studies have over-emphasized 'leadership' at the expense of 'management' – our own experience suggests that these are both important characteristics of the effective school – but they do underline the cultural significance of this term for teachers. Most recently, studies of leadership in schools have tended to move away from the identification of this function exclusively with the head teacher, and have begun to address how leadership can be made available throughout the management structure and at all levels in the school community. This shift in emphasis has been accompanied by a shift in thinking about leadership itself, with an increasing call for 'transformational' approaches which distribute and empower, rather than 'transactional' approaches which sustain traditional (and broadly bureaucratic) concepts of hierarchy and control.

One consequence of this shift in thinking is the realization in many schools that management arrangements may need to be modified or revised so that leadership can be more widely exercised. Leadership and management remain inextricably linked, but positive strategies for developing leadership approaches within the school and reflecting these in management structures are needed.

This chapter presents some activities which will help the school to scrutinize its current thinking about and practice of leadership. Inevitably, some aspects of what is an extremely complex process have been excluded. Thus, for example, we do not offer materials for exploring the link between leadership and the patterns and quality of communication, though this is clearly an important one. We have, however, selected aspects of the leadership function which have seemed in our own work to influence both the impact of leadership on the school community and the perceptions of leadership held by staff. This last point is important, because we have often been made aware (as external agents) that perceptions vary (sometimes significantly) both between levels and groups within the school, and between 'objective' analyses of leader behaviour and the way staff feel.

The activities which follow are, therefore, an attempt to bring together those aspects of leadership which the IQEA project schools have found most helpful in promoting school improvement, with those areas of school life where we have been most aware of the need for developments in leadership approach. The activities highlight the following aspects of leadership:

- the role of leadership in establishing a clear and agreed vision for the school
- the leadership skills involved in recognizing task-relevant expertise and in harnessing this to promote school improvement work
- the balance needed between work group cohesion and critical thinking, and the leader's role in retaining this balance
- the desirability of involving as many members of staff as possible in the leadership process, spreading responsibilities and widening empowerment.

Activity 8.1: Vision Building

Context

School improvement activities need to be guided by a vision of what is intended. Ideally this vision needs to be shared by all members of the school community. But, as one writer has suggested, the imposition of a vision onto a school by senior staff may actually interfere with the process of vision building. He refers to the notion of 'visions that blind'.

However, it is equally the case that without some kind of stimulus, a school staff may not see the articulation of a vision for the school as a major priority. It is therefore important that senior staff take a lead in the process of vision building, though what matters is that some 'plan' for drawing up or refining the key values and goals which unite staff is available, rather than specific direction as to what such values and goals should be. The current pressure for reforms from outside the school makes this a particularly opportune time to reconsider the school's vision, as without deliberate action from inside the school to safeguard its own values and priorities there is a real danger that external forces will drive the school. School leaders should therefore be seeking to establish active vision building through a participatory approach which allows for contributions from staff at all levels.

Briefing

Aims

- To provide an opportunity for staff members to reflect on the 'vision' or purposes which drive the school's efforts.

- To consider the role played by school leaders in the development of the school's vision, and the ways in which leadership can help link together whole school vision and individual action.

Process

This activity is structured in two or four parts, intended for use with small (approximately four to six members) groups of staff. Step 1 invites the group to consider how far the school's vision is revealed in its working practices on a day-to-day basis. In asking the group to take that external perspective it is hoped that this will encourage members to look for outward signs of particular goals, values and beliefs, rather than addressing these at the level of intentions. This exercise needs sufficient time to allow for a considered response. It may be useful to have copies of the school's vision or aims statement available to be fed into the discussions.

Step 2 invites the group to focus on the role leadership plays in creating the 'vision' and in focusing energies behind it. Depending on the time available and the number of groups taking part, it may be helpful to allow for the sharing of responses to Step 1. Similarly, it is possible to re-mix groups after Step 1, so that a comparison of different views can be made before the activity suggested for Step 2 is undertaken.

What is our vision?

Working in small groups consider what you might expect to read as an introductory description of the school in a forthcoming inspectors' report. In writing the description bear in mind the following questions:

• What would the report say about the working ethos of the school?

• What would it say about the quality of teaching and learning?

Step 2

Take the points identified in Step 1 and, for each, try to assess ways in which leadership in the school has contributed to the development of this aspect of the school.

Has leadership played a significant role in the development of school ethos and pupil–teacher relationships? What more could school leaders do in these areas?

Activity 8.2: Harnessing Individual Skills

Context

Central to any notion of effective leadership is the ability to identify and draw upon relevant knowledge, skills and experience. This is particularly important when groups are working together within the school, whether structural (e.g., senior management team) or task-related (e.g., a working party established to address a particular problem or issue). Research into group dynamics suggests that the performance of the group as a whole is often limited by the approach of the group leader. As schools become increasingly complex structures and more teachers gain opportunities to 'lead' a group of colleagues in some aspect of the school's activities, the need for individuals at all levels within the school who can assume a leadership role and bring the best out of colleagues has increased accordingly. Too frequently in such situations we are limited by stereotypes and by fixed ideas about the abilities of the work group. In fact, the capacity to engage in creative problem-solving is wide-spread, and we need to do more to ensure that we are drawing on this capacity when groups are convened. We also need to capitalize on the individual strengths of group members, using the available knowledge and skills to produce compound solutions which will often be better than we could produce from any one group member. This activity looks at how effectively we are able to make use of the different skills and abilities which individuals bring to working groups in the school, and explores the role of the group leader in promoting effective and rewarding work groups.

Briefing

Aims

- To promote discussion about the different skills and experiences available within the staff group, and the extent to which these are drawn on in the school's activities.

- To provide a format for exploring the effectiveness of working groups within the school.

- To help staff develop positive strategies for improving group effectiveness and for using the skills and experience of colleagues.

Process

This activity is divided into three parts. Steps 1 and 2 require individual reflection and note-making, and can either be carried out during or in preparation for an INSET session. The second stage (Step 2) involves the identification of factors contributing to group effectiveness, and we have found it useful to get staff to list these on a sheet of flipchart paper so that all participants are able to see one another's 'lists' during the plenary discussion which takes place in Step 3.

Step 1

Try to identify a work group of which you have been (are) a member, which you think has not used your knowledge and skills effectively in going about its tasks. Briefly list the reasons why you think the group has not made best use of you, and your feelings about this.

The reasons

My feelings

Step 2

Individually, identify a work group you have been (or are) a member of, which you would consider effective.

List your reasons for identifying this as an effective group.

-
-
-
-
-
-
-

Briefly describe the way the group was led.

Can you identify links between the way the group was led and its effectiveness?

Step 3

Join together with two colleagues and compare your responses. Make a list of the links you have identified between leadership behaviour and group effectiveness.

Now reflect on the comments you made during Step 1. How far would the leadership behaviours you have identified as promoting group effectiveness resolve these difficulties?

Context

One of the most difficult aspects of leading a work group is building and maintaining cohesion while simultaneously encouraging individuals to retain and to contribute their own individual responses and ideas. Team-building approaches, emphasizing common goals and developing a socio-psychological climate within the team which reinforces behaviours directed towards these goals, have become an increasingly important part of staff development activity. Certainly, since schools have in the past frequently been places which nurtured multiple, and sometimes conflicting, goals, the identification of shared goals and priorities is an important leadership function.

Nevertheless, the dynamics of groups which develop a clear set of purposes and a strong sense of identity may also bring less desirable side effects. It is an irony of cohesiveness that the very forces which hold a group together and which create a climate in which all members can feel comfortable, secure and able to express their views freely, sometimes inhibit freedom of expression. Leading a group, therefore, requires that we remain aware of this danger and do not bring about a level of cohesiveness which begins to reduce members' ability to engage in critical thinking. Specifically, it requires the leader to maintain focus on finding the best solutions to problems, and not simply locating those solutions on which group members can most readily agree.

This activity offers a method of looking at the behaviours which lead to cohesiveness and to over-cohesiveness. It takes as its point of focus staff meetings (these can be formal or informal) as the behaviours themselves and the impact of leadership style on group behaviour are most readily available to the observer on these occasions.

Briefing

Aims

- To alert staff to the need to avoid 'over-cohesiveness' in groups so that creativity and critical thinking continue to be encouraged.

- To provide frameworks which can be used to analyse meetings in the school for signs of over-cohesiveness.

- To consider what kinds of advice to those who chair meetings would improve the quality of critical thinking.

Process

This exercise needs careful planning by individual participants and time needs to be set aside for planning and carrying through the first two stages.

If a number of staff are involved these may well need to be spread over a number of weeks. Steps 1 and 2 both involve observation of meetings which are a normal part of the school's routines. Though not essential, it is often helpful if the observer can find some way of feeding back findings directly to the group involved, as well as making notes which will contribute to the discussion of issues arising.

Step 3 involves individual reflection on these activities and Step 4 can be carried out at an INSET meeting, or perhaps a departmental meeting of all members of the department who have taken part. Before moving to the fourth stage of this exercise (producing an 'Advice sheet'), it may be helpful to conduct a 'brainstorming' session.

Step 1

Looking for behaviours which inhibit critical thinking

Janis (1982) has suggested a range of behaviours which arise only in highly cohesive groups and which displace critical thinking by a desire to find agreement at all costs. Use the schedule on the next page to record the incidence of these behaviours in a meeting which you have arranged to observe. You should identify the participants along the top row of the matrix, and each time a particular participant contributes, ask yourself whether this contribution can be described by one of the behaviours listed down the left-hand side of the schedule. If you do 'recognize' one of these behaviours, put a mark in the relevant box in the matrix.

After the observation has been completed summarize your findings and make brief notes on points of interest.

Summary of Findings

Group Observation Schedule

Participants / Behaviours							
Stereotyping of outsiders							
Assuming moral superiority over outsiders							
Assuming win/lose situation							
Pressurizing a colleague to agree							
Pressing for unanimity							
Withholding information that might change the course of the discussion							

Step 2

Those who study the dynamics of groups have identified a range of behaviours which tend to be associated with effective group performance. These include:

- Clarifying the group's goals, so that all members understand these. Modifying and re-defining goals where necessary so that these reflect the understandings and individual goals of members.
- Establishing parity between group members, so that during discussions all members are able to participate fully and can assume a leadership role when appropriate.
- Ensuring that authority (position-based) does not become a more important factor than information (knowledge-based) in decision making.
- Drawing on a range of decision-making processes, rather than trying to 'standardize' the way the group approaches decisions. This allows for a matching of decision-approach with type of issue.
- Exploring differences and being prepared to engage in conflict. The group is committed to *resolving* conflict rather than *avoiding* it.
- Communication is open, and members are encouraged to express feelings and speculations as well as 'facts'.
- Group members reflect from time-to-time on the way the group is operating, evaluating its effectiveness and making changes in methods and approaches where necessary.

Arrange to observe a group in action (if possible the same group studied during Step 1 but on a different occasion).

During the observation look for examples of the above behaviours, noting:

1. Who engaged in the behaviour

2. What impact the behaviour had on the groups

Step 3

Following the observation make a brief summary recording any points of interest.

• Summary

• Points of interest

Step 4

Join together with the other participants in the observation exercise.

1. Compare and discuss findings from Step 1 and identify any common barriers to critical thinking.
2. Compare and discuss findings from Step 2, identifying those behaviours which seem to be most frequently associated with group effectiveness.
3. In light of your discussions, produce an 'Advice sheet' for those in the school who lead or chair groups. The advice sheet should focus on behaviour to be encouraged or avoided, and fit onto one side of A4.
4. Circulate your advice sheet to all members of staff, inviting further comment/suggestions.

© IQEA – Creating the Conditions for School Improvement

Context

Schools have often been described as 'loosely-coupled' organizations. In such organizations where the work of the individual teacher is carried out (for the most part) alone, and in classrooms which have been deliberately shut off from one another, there will always be difficulty in ensuring that individual effort is consistently placed behind organizational priorities. Leadership has a key role to play in aligning these two, but there is a choice about how leadership is applied. Often, leadership has been seen as a mechanism for controlling individual behaviour – imposing structures and rules, establishing a hierarchy for decision making and retaining central direction through prescription. Though such an approach can result in coordinated effort, it may also be wasteful of the individual's intellectual and problem-solving abilities, and is likely to reduce the school's capacity to respond quickly and flexibly to new situations.

More recently, leadership has been seen as an enabling rather than a controlling variable. In such a school, collective effort is put into defining and communicating priorities, and individuals are then invited to use their own knowledge and skills in making decisions which move the school in these directions. Essentially, the school is held together by a shared set of ideas and objectives rather than by structures. This approach empowers staff and allows participation in leadership at all levels in the school.

This activity will help the school to review its current approach to leadership and to establish whether there is a perception amongst staff that leadership is a function in which many have a share, or is vested in a few individuals in the most senior positions.

Briefing

Aims

- To help staff explore the range of perspectives on leadership held at different levels in the school organization.

- To identify opportunities for sharing the leadership function amongst staff in the school.

Process

This activity is organized into five stages. Steps 1 and 2 require staff to carry out 'interviews' with colleagues who work at different levels within the school, and to compare and contrast their findings. Specimen 'Interview schedules' are provided, but participants should feel free to develop their own or (at least) add their own questions to those suggested. Schedules have been drawn up for three 'levels' of staff: senior and middle management and class teacher. If the school is small, then the middle management level may not be applicable. Participants should modify their approach according to school circumstances.

Steps 1 and 2 need to be planned and carried through individually in preparation for Steps 3, 4 and 5 which are designed to take place in a plenary session. The third and fourth stages involve small groups (three or four teachers) and the final stage is a sharing of findings and proposals with the whole staff group.

On Appendix pp. 135–8 are three 'Interview schedules' which can be used to explore the different perspectives on leadership which exist in the school. These are labelled senior management, middle management and class teacher, and provide a basis for comparing the perspectives on leadership and perceptions about the way leadership is being used at the different levels within the school. It is possible, of course, to interview all members of staff, but the main aim of this exercise is to provoke thinking and discussion, rather than to 'analyse' the range of leader behaviour in the school.

Step 1

Select two colleagues, one from each of the groupings indicated on the schedules other than your own. (i.e., if you are a 'middle manager', choose a member of senior management and a class teacher; if you are a class teacher choose one representative from middle management and one from senior management, etc.). Using the schedules and, if you wish, adding questions of your own in the 'space' provided, carry out interviews with these two colleagues.

Step 2

Compare the perspectives and perceptions gathered in these interviews with your own, making brief notes on any differences and clear points of agreement.

Differences

Points of agreement

Step 3

Join with two colleagues and discuss your findings. In particular try to establish:

• whether there are common perceptions of the way leadership operates in the school
• whether senior and middle managers are aware of how their leadership style is perceived by others
• whether individuals feel they are given enough opportunity to share in the leadership process.

Step 4

Staying in groups of three, try to identify areas of school life where change is desirable and mechanisms for increasing the participation of staff in the leadership process.

Areas of development

Mechanisms for development

© IQEA – Creating the Conditions for School Improvement

Step 5

Report back to the staff group. List any points emerging from the discussion which either you or others should follow up at a later stage.

CHAPTER 9

The Journey of School Improvement

We often use the metaphor of 'the journey' to describe our work with the schools involved in the IQEA project. The image of the journey captures well the non-prescriptive and investigative nature of our collaboration. There is however another, perhaps more important, aspect to our approach to school improvement as a journey. The image was beautifully captured by the head of a secondary school recently, when he said at one of our meetings that, 'we journey as pilgrims, not as nomads'. What he was so evocatively reminding us of was that our collaborative approach to school improvement was based on a set of values that had characterized and disciplined our work together. So although we had all rejected the 'blueprint' or 'top-down' approach to change, we were not lurching from 'fad to fad' on a whim or impulse. Rather we were journeying in a direction that was, although not always well signposted, informed by goals, by a process, and by a vision that reflected a core set of values.

So what does the journey of school improvement look like in practice? Although there are many faces to success we have noted some patterns and trends which we believe can apply to other schools and other systems. A key finding from the early phase of the project was that *school improvement works best when a clear and practical focus for development is linked to simultaneous work on the internal conditions within the school*. Such school improvement efforts include:

- reconstructing externally imposed education reforms in the form of school *priorities*;
- creating *internal conditions* that will sustain and manage change in schools.

At times of great change, of innovation overload, schools need to be able not only to prioritize between competing policy or innovation objectives, and adapt these changes to the needs and aspirations of the school, but also to create the internal conditions for so doing. In order to illustrate this point we briefly describe the experiences of some schools involved in IQEA.

Example 1

> Subject departments in a secondary school wanted to introduce inductive teaching into their lessons. The technique involves the analysis of data-sets by students. A number of teachers in each department volunteered to teach using the technique, and reported back to colleagues and to the IQEA coordinating group in the school. The head made time available for other teachers to observe lessons, and through discussion, peer observation and peer coaching, the technique was disseminated throughout the school. When all staff felt confident to teach inductively, the technique was written into appropriate parts of each department's scheme of work.

Example 2

> An upper school which has been a member of the IQEA Project for a number of years has evolved a system for school-based research based upon cross-curricular task groups. These groups can involve up to half of the teaching staff in any single year. They also include students who have been trained in research methods, and who have been involved in the process of identifying areas for development within the school. Each group is allocated a budget which it can use at its own discretion. Some groups use it to buy supply cover to release colleagues to undertake classroom observation and research. The research activities are coordinated by a small cadre group which includes teachers at all levels of the school's management structure, including newly-qualified staff. Recent areas for research have included initial teacher training provision at the school, optimum seating arrangements for students and effective teaching strategies. The task groups are given regular opportunities to feed back any findings to the rest of the staff.

Example 3

> Two members of staff of a medium-sized secondary school were invited to lead an initiative on the *pace of learning*. This priority was identified as a result of an inspection of the school. Since neither teacher was a senior member of staff they chose initially to work with small groups of staff rather than go for whole-staff involvement at the outset. Working with colleagues in pairs they carried out classroom observation in order to collect data about existing practice, and to develop curriculum materials and teaching strategies designed to enhance the 'pace of learning'. Gradually they involved more teachers in their activities, and as a result the development work began to have an impact across the school. Time was allocated so that staff could work in one another's classroom in supporting development activities. Towards the end of the year staff who were involved in this classroom research presented some of their experiences during a whole-staff development day.

In each of these examples the schools, by linking together priorities and conditions, were increasing their capacity for handling change.

- The first cameo is a particularly good example of how head teachers can support colleagues by allocating the most valuable resource that teachers need – time. By providing cover so that colleagues could observe each other teaching, the head teacher demonstrated commitment to their professional development and to the improvement of the school.
- The second story shows how carefully organized task groups can foster a common understanding of educational issues which affect the whole school. The cross-hierarchical composition of each group, and the involvement of students, mean that the raising of educational issues, and the process of educational change, is not dependent upon the whim of senior management. The school in this cameo is truly a community of learners.
- The third example illustrates the 'think big start small' approach to change. As the coordinators and senior staff reflected on the changes in teaching styles that had occurred as a result of this work, they recognized a number of key strategies. The school had successfully reviewed and adapted certain conditions to support staff in their development tasks. The provision of time to work on the development group was a significant factor. In addition, the skills of the two coordinators in maintaining momentum and disseminating the work was important. Their decision to find ways of involving students was also recognized as a major strength in their activities.

The examples also demonstrate that school improvement is holistic rather than a fragmented process. But where does the journey of school improvement start? As the eastern mystic said, each long journey starts with a single footstep. And though ideally we may not choose to start from where we are, there is little to be gained by waiting until 'things' improve. In our experience they rarely do, at least by themselves. Although the metaphor of the journey implies an organic process, there does appear to be a number of distinct phases that schools go through during school improvement work. The nature of the work implied by each of these will obviously vary from school to school. At times phases may co-exist, or be entered in an order different from the somewhat linear description we give below. But despite this we know of no schools which have been successful in their development work that have not, at some time or the other, worked within each of these phases. Consistent with the metaphor of the journey we describe each of these phases in the form of a question:

Where are we now?
Where do we want to be?
How will we get there?
What do we need to do?
Where will we go next?

In Table 9.1 we identify the two key tasks in each phase.

Table 9.1 – Key questions for school improvement

Phase of the School Improvement Journey	Key Tasks
Where are we now?	• review the internal conditions of the school • encourage involvement in development work
Where do we want to be?	• discuss the school's 'vision' • identify priorities for development
How will we get there?	• consider implications for classroom practice • plan for action
What do we need to do?	• keep the momentum going • check regularly on progress
Where will we go next?	• move from one cycle of development to another • establish a development structure

Where are We Now?

The major theme of this book is the creation within the school of those internal conditions that support change. It is therefore helpful to take this as a key starting point. We encourage schools to review their conditions early on in their school improvement journeys. Sometimes it is necessary to concentrate much more in the initial stages on improving the conditions in the school and limit work on the priorities. Activities designed to assess the internal conditions of the school can also be used to generate awareness and build commitment towards development work.

The building of 'ownership' and making everyone aware of, if not involved in, school improvement is a vital early task. Of course the ultimate goal is to involve the whole school in development work. Early in the IQEA project we designed a rating scale to assist schools to *'review their internal conditions'*. The scale also helps to establish a common language within the school to discuss development strategies. The early feedback from collaborating schools convinced us that some (relatively straightforward) instrument, which could help schools diagnose their internal conditions with regard to school improvement, would be useful.

The scale is based on the six conditions for school improvement described in previous chapters. There are four items for each condition drawn on the key ideas described in each of the conditions chapters; this gives 24 items in all. A version of the scale (which is photo-copiable and copyright free) is found in Appendix pp. 140–44. For a full description of the scale, how to administer and analyse it, along with findings from projects where it has been used, see Chapter 10.

The scale, besides assisting in assessing the school's internal conditions, can also be used to accomplish the other key task in this phase – *building commitment towards development work*. To help in this, we have produced another method of reviewing internal conditions which is even quicker to use and rapidly leads to focused discussion. In this activity, two statements about each condition are presented and individual members of staff are asked to identify where they think the school is between the two points. This exercise can be used as part of a staff meeting or training day to facilitate discussion on what aspects of the school's conditions the staff feel work needs to be done on. The *'Exploring conditions that support school development'* discussion activity is also found (again in photo-copiable and copyright free format) in the Appendix (pp. 145–7).

Both of these review techniques have proven to be most helpful starting points. They give a picture of a school's ability to embark on development work, and generate interest within the school about improvement activities. They also lay a strong foundation for the next phase: deciding where the school wants to be.

Where do We Want to Be?

The two aspects of this phase involve discussion of the school's vision, and the identification of priorities for development. Given the emphasis in this book on creating the conditions for school improvement, we have sequenced this phase after the review of the conditions. Obviously we would not argue strenuously to maintain this strict chronological sequence. The sequencing of these two phases is less important than that they are both gone through.

Discussion of a school's 'vision' may make some readers uneasy and, possibly, cynical. Even to those who are comfortable with the concept there is a well founded suspicion that 'vision' is an artefact born of someone else's aspiration and handed down to the rest of us. That is not how we view 'vision'. Successful schools in our experience are characterized by a set of values which are shared by most staff and that guide the actions of those within the building. That is not to say that harmony and consensus are breaking out everywhere, but that most people share a perception of what the school stands for. As a head of a secondary school said to us recently, 'When there is general agreement on what we are about, then decision making is not really a problem'. This accords with our definition of vision: a philosophy that influences and underscores most people's actions within the school.

We reject the idea of vision as a given, an absolute. So rather than 'having a vision' it is far more important to engage in processes of 'vision building'. In this respect the head, although not the vision giver, has a key role to play in nurturing an overall vision for the school. In one secondary school, for example, the head-teacher occasionally holds meetings of the whole staff during which he muses about his views on important educational ideas. Staff members report that this helps them see their own work within a broader picture of where the school is going. Similarly, in an infant school, teachers refer to the head teacher's habit of 'thinking aloud' about policy matters as she mixes informally with the staff. Again, this seems to help individuals as they too think about overall school policy.

Although these are important and symbolic activities, we feel that in general it is counter-productive to spend too much time in discussing values in isolation from action. In the same way as changes to the culture of a school are not achieved by talking, but rather by working together on 'real' tasks, so vision is built by taking tangible steps to move the school forward. That is why we have linked together in this phase both vision building and deciding on developmental priorities. It is through the practical task of identifying developmental priorities, and then working on them, that the school's vision is secured.

The second aspect of this development phase then, is *identifying priorities for development*. In recent years development planning has become an important strategy for school improvement. Planning involves the school in generating a number of 'priorities' for action – often too many to work on. This means that decisions about the sequencing of 'priorities' must be made. Three principles should guide this process of choice among priorities:

- *manageability* – realistically, how much can we hope to achieve?
- *coherence* – is there a sequence which will ease implementation?
- *consonance* – how well do internally identified priorities coincide or overlap with external pressures for reform?

Schools that are able to see externally generated changes as providing opportunities, as well as (or instead of) problems, are better able to respond to 'top-down' demands. In IQEA, therefore, schools are encouraged to review, and in some cases to reconsider, their own priorities, as well as their conditions, at the outset of the project. As well as meeting the criteria for priorities outlined in Chapter 2, we ask schools in the project to:

- define for themselves an area or issue to be tackled;
- ensure that this is not a 'new' or 'additional' activity undertaken simply because of involvement in the project, but a real issue, problem or opportunity which the school needs to work on anyway;
- consider how this can be tackled in a way which develops the school and moves it some way towards the external requirements (stemming from national reforms) for quality improvement and assurance facing all schools;
- communicate this to all staff in the school.

In this latter regard, it is most desirable that there is a high level of agreement about the priorities among all the school's partners. A clear and explicit rationale helps people to reach agreement and explains why some of the possible priorities cannot be included at this time.

In *The Empowered School* (Hargreaves and Hopkins, 1991, pp. 42-4), four criteria for sequencing priorities are suggested:

- *Consider urgency, need and desirability.* Are some priorities, such as the legal requirements of the National Curriculum, urgent or unavoidable? Other possible priorities will be proposed because they are needed, while others may be desirable but less pressing.
- *Estimate size and scope.* Can some larger priorities, such as the National Curriculum or cross-curricular provision, be best divided into a series of annual 'chunks'? Priorities which extend over two or more years need very careful planning and management.

- *Distinguish between root and branch innovations.* Do some priorities provide strong roots, for example, a well-designed staff development policy, to support the branches of innovation which represent its growth from existing practice? School improvement involves two kinds of change: *root innovations* that generate the base on which other, or *branch innovations*, can be sustained.
- *Forge links between priorities.* Can priorities be chosen that are closely related to one another? This fosters collaboration between staff working on different targets and leads to greater progress.

By going through the process of identifying priorities the school is also establishing a dialogue or debate on the values that are important to it and its partners. As we have already intimated, successful schools appear to be those that live out a relatively coherent set of values. They are not 'givens' but develop as a result of debate and action, usually on issues of real substance and importance. Equally important as reviewing conditions, developing vision and identifying priorities, is putting them all together in an achievable plan. This is the topic of the next section.

How will We Get There?

The two key tasks here are the linking together of the work of the previous two phases on the conditions and priorities, together with an emphasis on classroom practice within the context of an action plan.

Our argument is that if development work is to have an impact on student outcomes then it needs to focus on *classroom practice*, as well as the internal conditions of the school. This point is well illustrated in the examples given at the beginning of the chapter where the teachers focused not only on development strategies, but also on active student learning, classroom-based research, and the pace of learning. In all of these examples, however, the action was fitted into some form of a plan.

Action planning is more than just listing a set of priorities. It involves creating a plan that is sufficiently detailed to assist colleagues in the day-to-day practical events of the journey. The plan should also be sufficiently flexible to allow mid-course corrections that result from the imaginative ideas that come to us as we engage deeply with our work, as well as, of course, those unanticipated events that inevitably occur. As some of our colleagues have recently phrased it: the message is not the classical 'Plan then do', but 'Do, then plan...and do and plan some more'.

We have already described aspects of planning in Chapter 4. As we saw there, plans need to be flexible guides to action, rather than blueprints. Action plans for teachers are very different from the development plan, which simply lists the school's priorities and as such is a relatively 'glossy' public document that is made available to a wider audience. Action plans are working documents for groups of teachers that link departmental and school priorities to classroom practice. Each action plan describes, preferably on one side of A4, the programme of work to be undertaken. It contains (Hargreaves and Hopkins, 1991, p. 51):

- the *priority* as described in the school's development plan;
- the *targets*, or the more specific objectives for the priority;
- the *success criteria* against which progress and success in reaching targets can be judged;

- the *tasks* or work to be undertaken to reach each target: there are tasks for both implementation and evaluation;
- the *allocation of responsibility* for targets and tasks, with time-lines;
- the dates for meetings *to assess progress*;
- the *resource* implications (materials and equipment, finance, INSET, etc.).

Focusing development work on classroom practice, and underpinning this with a feasible and realistic plan are necessary, but not sufficient, conditions for student achievement. Now is the time to move into action.

What do We Need to Do?

So far much of the discussion has been about preparation and planning. It is at this point that attention needs to be paid to action. The inevitable time lag between this and previous phases should be made as short as possible, if momentum is not to be lost. Similarly progress needs to be sustained during implementation. Schools also need to evaluate how they are doing. If implementation and evaluation are linked, evaluation can help to shape and guide the action plan rather than being a *post mortem* upon it.

Keeping the momentum going is a key task. After all the work of planning, it is easy to assume that an action plan, once agreed, will somehow look after itself. Yet our experience suggests that implementation does not proceed on automatic pilot! Successful implementation needs continual support. The enthusiasm of even the most committed staff can flag when routine work and unanticipated events distract teachers from the action plan. Senior staff, for example, can boost motivation and so sustain commitment by showing interest, making themselves accessible, and by involving themselves fully in development work.

Implementing action plans can be a hazardous journey, since progress often proceeds in fits and starts. When problems do occur, it is important to search for solutions rather than despair. The DES booklet, *Planning for School Development* (1989, p. 16) suggests some useful tactics:

- providing extra support to the affected team;
- re-assigning roles and responsibilities within the team;
- drawing upon the skills and experience of new members of staff;
- seeking additional outside help;
- modifying the projected time-scale;
- scaling down the planned action to more manageable proportions.

Circumstances may also change for the better and advantage can be taken of unforeseen opportunities to advance the rate of progress.

The DES booklet (1989) also has some helpful advice on *checking regularly on progress*. As we saw in Chapter 4, a *progress check* is an act of evaluation in the course of implementation. It is a response to the question: how are we doing so far? Many progress checks involve teachers using their professional experience to make an intuitive judgement on how well things are going. This is a natural part of monitoring one's activities. It becomes more systematic if these intuitive judgements are backed by evidence and shared within the team. We suggest that at least once a term progress on each task is checked against the success criteria associated with the target. The team will need some clear evidence of the extent of progress: if such *evidence* is recorded, the workload at a later stage will be reduced.

Success checks take place at the end of the developmental work on a target; their purpose is to check the success of implementation. The team now decides how successful the implementation of the target or priority as a whole has been. Checking success need not be complex or time-consuming. It will consist largely in collating, and then drawing a conclusion about, the earlier progress checks.

Although many schools find it quite straightforward to move into action, sustaining momentum during implementation, and especially monitoring progress, often prove far more difficult. Yet success in this phase is essential if the whole process is to be effectively institutionalized and the final stage reached.

Where will We Go Next?

The key activities at this important phase of the process are moving from one developmental cycle to another, and establishing a development structure within the school. Unless schools have developed this capacity, school improvement cannot be taken for granted.

As a school moves into *subsequent cycles of development*, new priorities must be identified and planned for. This cannot however be done in any mechanical way. The content of the new development plan will be shaped by factors, such as:

- priorities already established in previous planning sessions;
- any lessons learned from the original plan;
- any slow down or acceleration in progress;
- changes in national and local policies and initiatives;
- the school's long-term vision, which provides a guide as to how one set of priorities provide 'roots' or foundations for others;
- the changing needs and circumstances of the school.

Moving from one cycle to another is easier said than done. Schools often find it difficult to draw a line under certain developments and to move onto something new. It certainly helps to have a clear idea of what the school wants to achieve by when, and to build evaluation into the end of the work on a particular priority. What must be avoided is development work on a priority just 'fizzling out', and then the school searching around for something else to work on.

The transition from one cycle to another is greatly assisted by the creation of a *development structure*. Perhaps the most crucial challenge facing schools today is how to balance change and stability effectively: how on the one hand to preserve what is already successful in a school, and on the other, how to respond positively to innovation and the challenge of change. We believe that the school's internal conditions are crucial in achieving the correct balance. We are also realizing from our current work that by adapting their structural arrangements, many successful schools are finding it easier to move from one developmental sequence to another.

Schools are finding out quite rapidly, or eventually more painfully, that procedures established to organize teaching, learning and assessment cannot also cope with developmental activities which inevitably cut across established hierarchies, curriculum areas, meeting patterns, and timetables. What is required are complementary structures each with their own purpose, budget and ways of working. The innovative responses required for sustained development require:

- delegation;
- task groups;
- high levels of specific staff development;
- quality time for planning;
- collaborative classroom activity.

Obviously the majority of a school's time and resources will go on its day-to-day activities, but unless there is also an element dedicated to development then the school is unlikely to progress in times of change. Decisions can then be made as to what aspect of the school requires development, and it is that priority which gets the 'treatment' for a specified period of time. In practice, therefore, the development structure acts as a support system for the rest of the school's activities. A priority on teaching and learning, for example, will inevitably spread itself across a school's curriculum if carefully managed. After work on a particular development is completed, another aspect of the school's operation is selected, and so on. In time most aspects of the school will have been subject to some form of development activity.

It is in this way that schools respond effectively to the challenge of centralized imposed reform within a decentralized system. Schools will embrace some changes immediately. This will be because the school either has no other legal option, or because it has a particular expertise or penchant for that change. Other changes, where experience is perhaps lacking, are selected as development priorities and sequenced over time. Some centralized initiatives, however, are resisted, either because they are incompatible with the school's central purpose, or because they may just be wrong.

This discussion and the various examples given in this chapter go some way to responding to the question 'What is the process of school improvement in an era of change?'. Unless schools are able to take a more assertive approach towards external policy initiatives, they will continue to suffer from 'innovation overload' and gradually lose control of their own educational agenda. It is the integration of phases of action such as those described in this chapter into the daily life of the school that keeps the process of development going. We do not, however, view the evolving process of school improvement as a sequence of neat precise interlocking phases – real life is always more complex and unpredictable than that. But unless the activities implied by each of these phases become part and parcel of the school's *modus operandi* then the journey of school improvement will eventually lead into a *cul-de-sac*.

CHAPTER 10

Using the Conditions of School Rating Scale

The Purpose of the Rating Scale

The Conditions of School Rating Scale appears in Appendix 2. It consists of 24 behaviours related to the six conditions outlined in this book, and requires the school's management, teachers and support staff to comment upon their frequency. The purpose of this exercise is to:

- provide a broad-brush profile of the school's capacity to improve
- to provide schools with data to inform school-wide debate about their capacity to improve
- to provide baseline and interim data by which schools can measure the improvement of their conditions.

The Administration of the Scale

The scale is simple to administer. It asks staff to tick boxes attached to each statement according to whether they perceive that the particular behaviour occurs 'rarely', 'sometimes', 'often' or 'nearly always'. Whoever is administering the scale should stress that staff indicate whether they are managers, teachers or support staff. Responses are intended to be anonymous. This causes no problems where large numbers of staff are involved, but where there are small numbers, for example in Infants' schools, the administration needs to be handled with sensitivity. It may be best in such circumstances to allow someone who is not a staff member (for example a governor) to collate the data.

The scale is best administered when the various groups are meeting, for example at a whole staff meeting. The scale takes a maximum of 20 minutes to complete: the advantage of administering it when staff are together is that the return of all the scripts is guaranteed, and whoever is administering the scale does not waste valuable time in 'chasing up' recalcitrant staff members. If it is not possible to use a meeting in this way, then a clear deadline and a 'posting place' should be specified.

Collating the Data

Scripts, once collected, should be organized into management, teacher and support staff piles. You should discard any scripts where the status of the staff member has not been indicated. If you are collating data from a large

Secondary school, you could be dealing with close to 100 scripts, so allow at least two hours to complete the analysis.

Responses should be tallied on a simple tally chart which enables an analysis to be made for each of the 24 behaviours. An example of such a chart used by the IQEA Research Officer is included in Appendix 2.

Scores under each heading should be collated for each category of staff. Data can be presented in a number of ways.

- Add all the 'rarely' scores for each condition (e.g. 1.1–1.4, Reflection and Inquiry), followed by all the 'sometimes', 'often' and 'nearly always' responses for the same condition. Convert each total into a percentage of all responses (number of staff x 4). The data can then be presented in the form as illustrated in Figure 10.1. This highlights for schools the general areas which they feel may need further development. In the worked example, the behaviours relating to the 'Involvement' condition appear to occur less frequently than those related to the other conditions.

THE CONDITIONS OF SCHOOL

_____ SCHOOL

SUMMARY SHEET: WORKED EXAMPLE

	Rarely	Sometimes	Often	Nearly Always
Reflection and Inquiry	3% (13)	28% (105)	35% (131)	34% (126)
Planning	4% (14)	28% (101)	45% (167)	23% (85)
Involvement	10% (37)	41% (142)	40% (140)	9% (32)
Staff Development	2% (8)	24% (85)	46% (164)	28% (101)
Coordination	6% (20)	33% (117)	43% (152)	18% (65)
Leadership	3% (13)	25% (90)	47% (174)	25% (90)

Figure 10.1 Data Presentation as Percentages of Total Responses (reproduced from Ainscow _et al._, 1994: 57)

- Add all the 'rarely' to all the 'sometimes' scores for each condition, and then all the 'often' scores to all the 'nearly always' scores for each condition. Convert these into percentages of the total responses. This approach has been used by IQEA in the past to give schools some idea of the state of their conditions in comparison to other schools in the same project. Figure 10.2 compares the percentages of teacher responses in the 'often' and 'nearly always' categories for the Staff Development condition in 18 Nottinghamshire IQEA schools in 1998. This helped LEA officers involved in the project to identify schools where staff development was an issue. School 14, which scored comparatively low on all six conditions, was identified as being in need of a considerable LEA intervention.

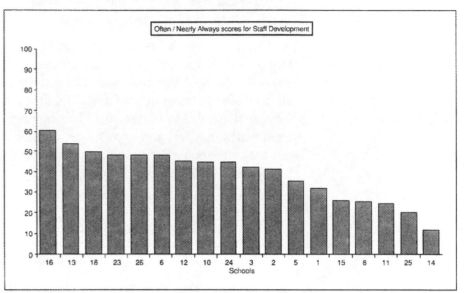

Figure 10.2 Staff Development condition in 18 Nottinghamshire schools, 1998

• During the 1990s, schools became increasingly interested in responses to individual statements in the scale. We therefore started to provide Likert scores for each statement. This involves scoring each 'rarely' response as 1, 'sometimes' as 2, 'often' as 3 and 'nearly always' as 4. This new total is then divided by the number of respondents to each statement, and a table like that in Figure 10.3 can be provided for individual schools. Scores of 1.0–2.0 suggest that behaviours occur comparatively rarely, scores of 2.1–2.9 that they occur occasionally, and scores of over 3 that they occur as a matter of course. The table format enables schools at a glance to note differences in response to individual statements by different categories of employee.

General Findings

Having administered the conditions scale to over 200 schools over a period of 6 years, we can make the following generalization about the data we have collected:

• Senior managers have a 'rosier' view of the management conditions in their school than other categories of staff. That is, they feel that behaviours generally occur more often than the teachers and support staff in their schools. This is unsurprising, given that they spend a large part of the school day managing.
• Teachers are more critical of the management conditions than support staff, whose views are closer to those of managers.
• The 'involvement' condition is consistently the one with the lowest responses. For example, a combined percentage score of over 50 per cent for 'often' and 'nearly always' responses is exceptionally rare.

			Teachers 1026	Managers 227	Support Staff 240
Inquiry	1.1	In this school we talk about the quality of our teaching.	2.5	2.8	2.8
	1.2	As a school we review the progress of changes we introduce.	2.4	2.6	2.6
	1.3	Teachers make time to review their classroom practice.	2.3	2.3	2.5
	1.4	The school takes care over issues of confidentiality.	3.2	3.5	3.4
Planning	2.1	Our long-term aims are reflected in the school's plans.	3.0	3.4	3.0
	2.2	In our school the process of planning is regarded as being more important than the written plan.	2.3	2.6	2.4
	2.3	Everyone is fully aware of the school's development priorities.	2.6	2.9	2.4
	2.4	In the school we review and modify our plans.	2.7	3.0	2.7
Involvement	3.1	In this school we ask students for their views before we make major changes.	1.8	1.8	1.9
	3.2	This school takes parents' views into consideration when changes are made to the curriculum.	1.9	1.9	2.1
	3.3	Governors and staff work together to decide future directions for the school.	2.2	2.7	2.8
	3.4	We make effective use of outside support agencies in our development work.	2.2	2.5	2.6
Staff Development	4.1	Professional learning is valued in this school.	2.6	3.1	2.9
	4.2	In devising school policies emphasis is placed on professional development.	2.3	2.8	2.6
	4.3	In this school the focus of staff development is on the classroom.	2.4	2.7	2.8
	4.4	The school's organization provides time for staff development.	2.1	2.7	2.5
Coordination	5.1	Staff taking on coordinating roles are skilful in working with colleagues.	2.5	2.7	2.7
	5.2	We get tasks done by working in teams.	2.6	2.9	2.7
	5.3	Staff are kept informed about key decisions.	2.4	3.1	2.5
	5.4	We share experiences about the improvement of classroom practices.	2.2	2.4	2.4
Leadership	6.1	Staff in the school have a clear vision of where we are going.	2.4	2.7	2.4
	6.2	Senior staff delegate difficult and challenging tasks.	2.3	2.4	2.4
	6.3	Senior management take a lead over development priorities.	2.8	3.1	2.8
	6.4	Staff are given opportunities to take on leadership roles.	2.2	2.7	2.3

Figure 10.3 National Norms for Conditions Scale

We have calculated Likert scores for each statement for 29 schools mainly in Nottinghamshire, Bedfordshire and Swansea. The average scores for each statement and each category of staff are presented in Figure 10.3. This enables you to compare your own school's scores with what we are developing as national 'norms'.

The Lessons of the Conditions Scale

Our hope is that the use of the conditions scale will generate a debate within your school about some of the discrepancies, contrasts and issues thrown up in the analysis. Below are some case studies of how some of our IQEA Project schools used their scale data to improve their schools.

Vignette 1 – Involvement of students in the curriculum

A small comprehensive school in East Anglia had only three teaching staff in its Technology department, and was concerned about the restricted curriculum it was able to provide for students. Timetabling requirements meant that students had all their three Technology lessons on the same day. The department itself was concerned that the timetabling and the restricted curriculum being offered was colouring students' views of the subject, which would in turn impact upon option choices for GCSE. The school arranged for 40 students of various abilities in Years 8, 9 and 10 to be interviewed.

Boys in the school seemed more convinced than girls that technology was an important school subject. Only half of the Year 8 students gave unqualified support for it, and half of those interviewed of average ability across the three year-groups did not think it was important. The equipping with life skills was deemed slightly more important than the provision of skills for employment.

Boys' assessments of their own ability were higher than the girls'. Year 10 students had a higher opinion of their ability levels than their teachers had. 85 per cent of the students interviewed thought they were 'OK' or better at Technology – their teachers considered 50 per cent of them as average or above.

Girls, and students of average ability, did not on the whole enjoy Technology. Some felt unable to give blanket approval because they only liked parts of the subject. These seemed to be primarily the practical activities, in particular cooking for girls. A third of those interviewed, with a considerable concentration in Year 10, disliked theory and written work, which most lumped together. Boys of high ability wanted to do some metalwork. Nearly half of the girls wanted to do more cooking.

The animosity felt towards parts of what is a wide and academic curriculum requirement for GCSE Technology has led the school to consider, for some students, various course modules which allow for greater technical specialization without what these students and their teachers regard as an over-academic approach to the subject.

Vignette 2 – Planning and review

A comprehensive school in the north of England had streamed its Year 8 cohort into 3 bands – Higher, Middle and Foundation. The Higher band consisted of 3 setted classes (H1, H2 and H3), the Middle band of two setted classes (M1 and M2) and the Foundation band of one class. Concerned about under-achievement in the Middle band, the senior management of the school decided to canvass the views of the Middle band students on being where they were.

None of the 28 interviewed found the work uniformly difficult. About a third found it varied from subject to subject, another third found it pitched at about the right level. Most of them claimed to work hard in lessons. More interestingly, about half had ambitions to move into the Higher band, while the other half were content to stay put. None felt that there was any prospect of dropping into Foundation.

Those wishing to stay in the Middle band quoted friendships and the easiness of the work compared to that in the Higher band as the main factors. 'I'd rather be brainiest in a thicky class than have to move up', said one boy. Students were aware of the wide ability range in the Middle band, and some realised that doing well in the Middle band did not guarantee success in the Higher. 'I don't want to fail higher up', said one girl.

Those aspiring to the Higher band felt frustrated. Though there was movement within bands, it was common knowledge that only two or three students moved between bands each year. One plaintively testified that 'I try my hardest, but I can't get there'. There was some resentment expressed about the behaviour of the few in disrupting various lessons, which the aspirants saw as preventing them from getting good grades and therefore as 'holding them back'. In addition, some teachers were blamed for not keeping control of classes, and issues like homework not being marked were also seen as factors hindering the progress of individual students.

The views of the aspirant and non-aspirant groups were fortified by the respective mythologies which each had created about the Higher and Foundation bands. For those wanting to stay, the Higher band students got too much work, and the pace of work was too fast. For the aspirants, the Higher band got less homework, their classes were slightly smaller than Middle band ones, and they were being given a better chance than Middle band students.

The mythology about the Foundation band was shared. Some Foundation students couldn't write, their work was easier but they didn't try, and they had behavioural problems. Foundation band work was the same as Middle band work – it just took Foundation students longer to do it. Foundation and Higher band students called each other names.

The Middle band was thus equally split between a group with little prospect of relegation, fortified in its complacency by a fear of what promotion would bring, and a group with thwarted ambitions further frustrated by their perceptions of the promised land. The combination was a recipe for apathy and under-achievement. The research led to a review of setting within the school.

Vignette 3 – Providing leadership roles

A school in the Home Counties experienced student behavioural problems linked to a high level of truancy. It decided to address the issue of developing relationships for all students by employing a Schools Outreach teacher. This teacher was given a unique wandering brief, and no teaching commitments. As a member of the local community he was in a position to develop relationships with students both in and out of school. Staff regarded him as a valuable 'mop', 'sponge' and 'listening ear' for student concerns.

He was regarded as a friend by students, who called him by his first name. He had had personal contact with a fifth of the Year 11 cohort. He ran camps for students in Years 9 and 10.

Students felt comfortable in talking about him, and their relationship with him. They talked to him about their problems. One boy 'had felt angry about people', and 'he calmed me down'. Another testified that 'I only come to school because he's here'.

The attendance records of nearly all of the students with whom the Outreach teacher had dealings improved dramatically. The Outreach teacher, from being on a temporary contract, is now a permanent member of staff. He continues to provide for many the vital relationship with an adult which is necessary to the learning of all students.

> **Vignette 4 – Taking time to review classroom practice**
>
> A school in south-east England was concerned about its poor showing in the GCSE League Tables, and decided to address the issue of whether the teaching strategies employed by its staff were the most suitable for its particular students. It was therefore decided to map the various strategies used by teachers in a range of subjects, and to canvass the views of students on the teaching strategies which they preferred.
>
> Using an observation schedule and student questionnaire based upon the work of Kolb, six Year 8 lessons and four Year 10 lessons were observed. 79 Year 8 students and 23 Year 10 girls were asked to indicate their learning preferences.
>
> Humanities and Modern Language lessons showed a heavy bias in favour of didactic, teacher-centred classroom activities. One of the two Creative Arts lessons observed showed a similar bias, as did two of the three Science lessons. Overall, 80 per cent of the teaching strategies observed fell into this category, and only 20 per cent involved independent learning skills.
>
> In contrast, the students' preferences indicated a mix of teaching strategies consisting of 62 per cent didactic, and 38 per cent facilitating independent learning. Subsequent research in different schools suggests that this is by no means exceptional (Beresford 1999).
>
> Kolb and others argue that an over-use of a restricted range of teaching strategies disenfranchises large sections of students. Confronted with these findings, the school asked itself whether the National Curriculum lent itself to catering for a range of learning styles and, more pertinently, what part considerations of classroom control played in the choice of teaching methods employed by its staff.

These vignettes suggest that a scrutiny and discussion of the data derived from the conditions scale can generate further school-based research which can both enrich and explicate points raised in the survey. We do not claim that the conditions scale is 'rocket science' – indeed, we would argue that much of its content is based upon common sense and has, indeed, become entrenched in the workings of most schools since we first formulated it in 1994. We have not arrived at an 'optimum' profile for the perfect school which can be derived from the scale – we can only tell you that our 'vanguard' IQEA school, which has been in the project for some 10 years, was still only scoring just over 50 per cent for 'often' and 'nearly always' responses for the 'Involvement' condition in 1999. They feel that they are still very much on the 'journey'. What we feel to be the most important feature of the scale is that it gets staff talking about practice. And therein lies the key to school improvement.

Handout Sheets, OHT Masters and Materials for Activities in Chapters 3–8

Handout Sheet for Activity 4.2: Action Planning

Taking the lists of knowledge, attitudes, and skills identified, place these in rank order according to how influential you believe each will be in successfully implementing the change. Then consider how to bring each objective about: What action is required? By whom? What resources will be involved? What success criteria have been identified? When will the work be completed?

Objective	Action Required	By whom?	Resources Required	Success Criteria	Complete by

REGULAR PROGRESS CHECKS INVOLVE

- giving somebody in the team responsibility for ensuring that the progress checks take place

- reviewing progress at team meetings, especially when taking the next step forward or making decisions about future directions

- deciding what will count as evidence of progress in relation to the success criteria

- finding quick methods of collecting evidence from different sources

- recording the evidence and conclusions for later use

© DES (1989)

SOME PROGRESS CHECKS MAY SHOW THAT

- the time schedules were too tight

- circumstances have changed since the plan was constructed and unexpected obstacles have been encountered

- there is a loss of direction and some mid-course correction is required for the target to be met

SUCCESS CRITERIA

are a form of school-generated performance indicator which:

- give *clarity* about the target: what exactly are you trying to achieve?

- point to the *standard* expected by the team

- provide advance warning of the *evidence* needed to judge successful implementation

- give an indication of the *time-scale* involved

NINE STATEMENTS ABOUT PROFESSIONAL LEARNING

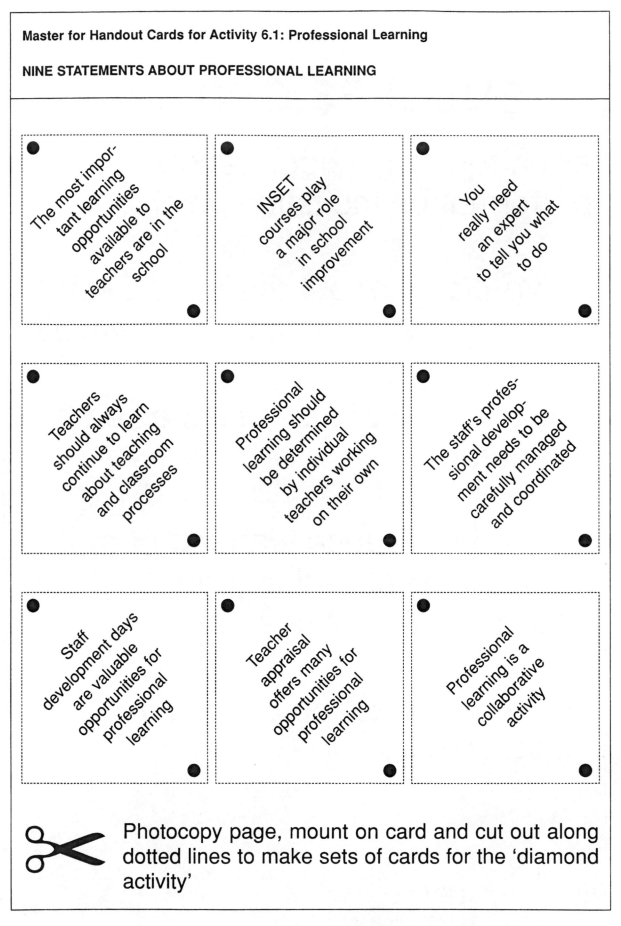

The most important learning opportunities available to teachers are in the school

INSET courses play a major role in school improvement

You really need an expert to tell you what to do

Teachers should always continue to learn about teaching and classroom processes

Professional learning should be determined by individual teachers working on their own

The staff's professional development needs to be carefully managed and coordinated

Staff development days are valuable opportunities for professional learning

Teacher appraisal offers many opportunities for professional learning

Professional learning is a collaborative activity

Photocopy page, mount on card and cut out along dotted lines to make sets of cards for the 'diamond activity'

Masters for Interview Schedules for Activity 8.4: Involving Staff in the Leadership Process

INTERVIEW SCHEDULE 1 – SENIOR MANAGEMENT

Q.1 How would you describe the head's/senior management's approach to leadership in the school? Can you illustrate this with reference to recent decisions in the school?

Q.2 Do you feel that there is a clear understanding by staff of the processes and mechanisms for decision making and the opportunities for participation in the management of the school?

Q.3 Are you aware of any tensions between the need for 'strong leadership' and the need for a sympathetic accommodation of individual viewpoints? Can you give examples of this?

Q.4 Can you give examples of different responses from individual members of staff to the same management approach – how would you account for this?

Q.5 What opportunities exist for middle managers to develop their leadership skills within the school – is there 'planned' development or does it depend upon individual initiative?

Q.6 Do you feel comfortable with the balance between managerial authority and professional autonomy in the school?

Q.7 How do you feel the approach to school leadership has changed during your own teaching career? How would you see it changing in the future?

Q.8 Do you believe that there is a style of leadership which works best in schools – if so, what is it, and how far is it innate rather than learned?

Q.9

Q.10

© IQEA – Creating the Conditions for School Improvement

Q.1 How would you describe the senior management's approach to leadership in the school? Can you illustrate this with reference to recent decisions in the school?

Q.2 Do you have a clear understanding of how decisions are made in the school? How would you describe your own opportunities to participate/influence?

Q.3 What opportunities are available for you to develop your own leadership skills? Do you feel you are given support/encouragement to experiment with leader behaviours within your department or area of responsibility?

Q.4 Do you find any tensions arising from your position as a member of the school's managerial structure on the one hand and as a representative of a professional grouping within the school on the other?

Q.5 Do you feel that you vary your approach to leadership according to the individual member of staff you are dealing with – if so can you give examples of and reasons for this?

Q.6 What constraints (if any) do you feel inhibit your leadership role within the department? How might these constraints be tackled?

Q.7 How, ideally, would you like to see the head of department's/middle manager's leadership role developed? How do you see it developing over the next five years?

Q.8

Q.9

INTERVIEW SCHEDULE 3 – CLASS TEACHERS

Q.1 How would you describe the senior management's approach to leadership in the school? Can you illustrate this with reference to recent decisions in the school?

Q.2 How would you describe the style of leadership in your department – can you give examples?

Q.3 Do you feel that you are given sufficient opportunities to participate/influence the management of your department?

Q.4 Do you feel that there is a satisfactory balance between managerial authority and professional autonomy within the school?

Q.5 How would you like to see leadership practices develop in schools?

Q.6 What opportunities are there/should there be for you to develop your own leadership skills in preparation for promotion within the school?

Q.7

Q.8

Q.9

The Conditions of School Rating Scale and Discussion Exercise for Chapter 9

THE CONDITIONS OF SCHOOL

RATING SCALE

Attached is a series of 24 statements about your school. We would like to know how far these statements match *your own* perception of the school, in other words, your *personal view* of it. There are no 'right' answers – we are seeking your opinion.

Please indicate your present post:

Support Staff	
Teacher	
Management Team	

(The rating scale and analysis advice on pp.140–44 are adapted from *Mapping Change in Schools: The Cambridge Manual of Research Techniques*)

ENQUIRY/REFLECTION				
1.1	In this school we talk about the quality of our teaching.			
	RARELY	SOMETIMES	OFTEN	NEARLY ALWAYS
1.2	As a school we review the progress of changes we introduce.			
	RARELY	SOMETIMES	OFTEN	NEARLY ALWAYS
1.3	Teachers make time to review their classroom practice.			
	RARELY	SOMETIMES	OFTEN	NEARLY ALWAYS
1.4	The school takes care over issues of confidentiality.			
	RARELY	SOMETIMES	OFTEN	NEARLY ALWAYS
PLANNING				
2.1	Our long-term aims are reflected in the school's plans.			
	RARELY	SOMETIMES	OFTEN	NEARLY ALWAYS
2.2	In our school the process of planning is regarded as being more important than the written plan.			
	RARELY	SOMETIMES	OFTEN	NEARLY ALWAYS
2.3	Everyone is fully aware of the school's development priorities.			
	RARELY	SOMETIMES	OFTEN	NEARLY ALWAYS
2.4	In the school we review and modify our plans.			
	RARELY	SOMETIMES	OFTEN	NEARLY ALWAYS
INVOLVEMENT				
3.1	In this school we ask students for their views before we make major changes.			
	RARELY	SOMETIMES	OFTEN	NEARLY ALWAYS
3.2	This school takes parents' views into consideration when changes are made to the curriculum.			
	RARELY	SOMETIMES	OFTEN	NEARLY ALWAYS
3.3	Governors and staff work together to decide future directions for the school.			
	RARELY	SOMETIMES	OFTEN	NEARLY ALWAYS
3.4	We make effective use of outside support agencies e.g., advisers and lecturers (in our development work).			
	RARELY	SOMETIMES	OFTEN	NEARLY ALWAYS

STAFF DEVELOPMENT			
4.1	**Professional learning is valued in this school.**		
	RARELY	SOMETIMES	OFTEN	NEARLY ALWAYS
4.2	**In devising school policies emphasis is placed on professional development.**		
	RARELY	SOMETIMES	OFTEN	NEARLY ALWAYS
4.3	**In this school the focus of staff development is on the classroom.**		
	RARELY	SOMETIMES	OFTEN	NEARLY ALWAYS
4.4	**The school's organization provides time for staff development.**		
	RARELY	SOMETIMES	OFTEN	NEARLY ALWAYS

COORDINATION			
5.1	**Staff taking on coordinating roles are skilful in working with colleagues.**		
	RARELY	SOMETIMES	OFTEN	NEARLY ALWAYS
5.2	**We get tasks done by working in teams.**		
	RARELY	SOMETIMES	OFTEN	NEARLY ALWAYS
5.3	**Staff are kept informed about key decisions.**		
	RARELY	SOMETIMES	OFTEN	NEARLY ALWAYS
5.4	**We share experiences about the improvement of classroom practice.**		
	RARELY	SOMETIMES	OFTEN	NEARLY ALWAYS

LEADERSHIP			
6.1	**Staff in the school have a clear vision of where we are going.**		
	RARELY	SOMETIMES	OFTEN	NEARLY ALWAYS
6.2	**Senior staff delegate difficult and challenging tasks.**		
	RARELY	SOMETIMES	OFTEN	NEARLY ALWAYS
6.3	**Senior management take a lead over development priorities.**		
	RARELY	SOMETIMES	OFTEN	NEARLY ALWAYS
6.4	**Staff are given opportunities to take on leadership roles.**		
	RARELY	SOMETIMES	OFTEN	NEARLY ALWAYS

© IQEA – Creating the Conditions for School Improvement

	Rarely	Sometimes	Often	Nearly Always
1.1				
1.2				
1.3				
1.4				
2.1				
2.2				
2.3				
2.4				
3.1				
3.2				
3.3				
3.4				
4.1				
4.2				
4.3				
4.4				
5.1				
5.2				
5.3				
5.4				
6.1				
6.2				
6.3				
6.4				

	Rarely	Sometimes	Often	Nearly Always
Enquiry and Reflection				
Planning				
Involvement				
Staff Development				
Coordination				
Leadership				

UNIVERSITY OF CAMBRIDGE INSTITUTE OF EDUCATION

IMPROVING THE QUALITY OF EDUCATION FOR ALL

Exploring conditions that support school development

Experience in the project schools over the last year has led us to reconstruct our typology of conditions for school improvement. Our current thinking is summed up by the following six rather general headings:

— Staff development
— Involvement
— Leadership
— Coordination
— Enquiry and reflection
— Planning

The attached sheets suggest extreme positions with respect to other areas of school life.

Tasks:

1. Indicate on each line your perception of your own school, (a) at the start of the year; and (b) currently.
2. Where you believe there has been movement make some notes as to what factors may have had an influence.

IQEA Condition 1: Staff Development

Staff development activities make little impact on classroom practice.	Staff development activities are leading to improvements in classroom practice.

....
....
....
....
....
....

IQEA Condition 2: Involvement

Pupils and parents feel that they have little opportunity to influence policy.	Pupils and parents are fully involved in policy discussions.

....
....
....
....
....
....

IQEA Condition 3: Leadership

Very few members of staff feel able to take a lead in school development activities.	All staff feel able to take a lead in school development activities.

....
....
....
....
....
....

IQEA Condition 4: Coordination

Staff are uncertain about priorities and plans, and how decisions are made.		Policies, plans and decision-making procedures are understood by all staff.

....
....
....
....
....
....

IQEA Condition 5: Enquiry and Reflection

Little use is made of data (e.g., classroom observations, test results) to inform planning and monitor progress.		Data are used to inform planning and monitor progress.

....
....
....
....
....
....

IQEA Condition 6: Planning

Staff are rarely involved in school planning processes.		Staff are fully involved in school planning processes.

....
....
....
....
....
....

References

Ainscow, M., Hargreaves, D. H., Hopkins, D., Balshaw, M. and Black-Hawkins, K. (1994) *Mapping Change in Schools: The Cambridge Manual of Research Techniques*. Cambridge: Institute of Education.

Beresford, J. (1999) 'Matching Teaching to Learning', *Curriculum Journal*, 10 (3), 321/344.

DES (1989) *Planning for School Development*. London: HMSO.

Hargreaves, D.H. and Hopkins, D. (1991) *The Empowered School*. London: Cassell.

Hopkins, D., Ainscow, M. and West, M. (1994) *School Improvement in an Era of Change*. London: Cassell.

Hopkins, D., West, M., Ainscow, M. Harris, A. and Beresford, J. (1997) *Creating the Conditions for Classroom Improvement*. London: David Fulton Publishers.

Janis, J. L. (1982) *Groupthink: Psychological Studies of Policy Decisions and Fiascoes,* 2nd edn. Boston: Houghton Mifflin College.

Wolfendale, S. (1987) *Primary Schools and Special Needs*. London: Cassell.

Suggested Further Reading

Barth, R. S. (1990) *Improving Schools from Within.* San Francisco: Jossey-Bass.

Beresford, J. (1998) *Collecting Information for School Improvement.* London: David Fulton Publishers.

Brighouse, T. and Woods, D. (1999) *How to Improve your School.* London: Routledge.

Caldwell, B. and Spinks, J. (1992) *Leading the Self-managing School.* London: Falmer Press.

Day, C., Harris, A., Hadfield, M., Tolley, H. and Beresford, J. (2000) *Leading Schools in Times of Change.* Buckingham: Open University Press.

Fielding, M., Fuller, A. and Loose, T. (1999) 'Taking Pupil Perspectives Seriously', in Southworth, G. and Lincoln, P. (eds) *Supporting Improving Primary Schools: The Role of Heads and LEAs in Raising Standards.* London: Falmer Press. Chapter 5.

Fullan, M. (1991) *The New Meaning of Educational Change.* London: Cassell.

Fullan, M. and Hargreaves, A. (1992) *What's Worth Fighting for in Your School?* Buckingham: Open University Press.

Gray, J., Hopkins, D., Reynolds, D., Wilcox, B., Farrell, S. and Jesson, D. (1999) *Improving Schools: Performance and Potential.* Buckingham: Open University Press.

Harris, A. (1999) *Effective Subject Leadership in Secondary Schools.* London: David Fulton Publishers.

Joyce, B., Wolf, J. and Calhoun, E. (1993) *The Self Renewing School.* Alexandria, VA: ASCD.

Joyce, B., Calhoun, E. and Hopkins, D. (1999) *The New Structure of School Improvement.* Buckingham: Open University Press.

Myers, K. (ed.) (1995) *School Improvement in Practice: Schools Make a Difference Project.* London: Falmer Press.

Rosenholtz, S. (1989) *Teachers' Workplace: The Social Organisation of Schools.* London: Longman.

Senge, P. (1990) *The Fifth Discipline: The Art and Practice of the Learning Organisation.* London: Century.

Southworth, G. (2000, in press) 'How Primary Schools Learn'. *Research Papers in Education* **15**(3).

Southworth, G. and Conner, C. (1999) *Managing Improving Primary Schools: Using Evidence-based Management and Leadership*. London: Falmer Press.

Stoll, L. and Fink, D. (1996) *Changing Our Schools: Linking School Effectiveness and School Improvement*. Buckingham: Open University Press.

West, M. and Ainscow, M. (1991) *Managing School Development*. London: David Fulton Publishers.

Index